The Book On Marketing For Assisted Living Facilities

How to Get More Tours, More Move-Ins, and More Success

Mitch Alverson

Copyright © 2022 Mitch Alverson

All rights reserved.

ISBN: 978-0-578-39836-5

DEDICATION

This book is dedicated to my lovely wife, Michele. Without her, I'd be a real mess. Thanks for helping me get through this thing called life. I love you and I love our family.

CONTENTS

Chapter 1: Your Online Marketing Plan   3

Chapter 2: Start with the Fundamentals   16

Chapter 3: How to Set Up Your Website   20

Chapter 4: Understand How Search Engines Work   31

Chapter 5: Search Engine Optimization   37

Chapter 6: Google Business Profile Optimization   54

Chapter 7: Website Conversion Fundamentals   71

Chapter 8: Mobile Optimization   82

Chapter 9: Social Media Marketing for ALFs   92

Chapter 10: Email Marketing for ALFs   108

Chapter 11: Maximize Your PPC   114

Chapter 12: Paid Online Directories   133

Chapter 13: Track, Measure, and Quantify   137

Chapter 14: What's Next   145

ACKNOWLEDGMENTS

I'd like to acknowledge all of the Assisted Living Facilities, Senior Communities, and Residential Care Homes who battled through the COVID-19. You are to be commended. Thanks for fighting. Thanks for caring.

1 YOUR ONLINE MARKETING PLAN (WEBSITE, SEO, PPC, ETC...)

Congratulations on your purchase of "The Book on Digital Marketing For Assisted Living Facilities: How to Get More Tours, More Move-Ins, and More Success," a complete overview of what it takes to maximize your opportunities online in terms of Leads, Calls, and Revenue.

There are a number of channels/mediums to consider for your facility when you look at the Online Marketing space. Whatever category your home or homes belong in, this book has the plan for you.

At first glance, considering all the marketing options available in your online marketing playbook might be overwhelming. These include Search Engines (Organic, Maps, Pay-Per-Click), Social Media (Facebook, Twitter, LinkedIn), Paid Online Directory Listings (A Place for Mom, Caring.com, BOTW, FourSquare, Yelp.com, etc.), and Paid Online Lead Services.

To maximize your lead flow from the Internet, you need to develop a PLAN which covers each of these online marketing opportunities. The purpose of this book is to outline a plan that will transform you from an online marketing novice to the dominant player in the Assisted Living Facility industry.

Throughout this book, we lay the foundation to:

- Map out your online marketing plan (Website, SEO, PPC, Pay-Per-Lead services, etc.)

- Start with the fundamentals (Market, Message, Media) before jumping headfirst into your Internet Marketing Strategy

- Setup your website

- Understand how search engines work, and learn the differences between the paid, organic, and map listings

- Optimize with Search Engine Optimization - How to optimize your website with keywords that are most important for your particular business

  - How to conduct keyword research

  - Our list of the most commonly searched keywords broken down by industry

  - How to achieve the maximum result by mapping out the pages which should be included on your website

  - How to optimize your website for ranking in the organic listings on major search engines

  - How to improve your website's visibility so you can rankon page one for your most important keywords

  - List of link building techniques and strategies that are proven to enhance rankings even in the post Penguin and Panda Era

- ○ Content marketing strategies for maintaining relevance in the Senior Living space

- Optimize Google Maps - How to get ranked on the Google Map in your area

  - ○ The fundamentals of Google Maps ranking (NAP, Citations, Consistency and Reviews)

  - ○ How to establish a strong name, address, and phone number profile

  - ○ How to properly claim and optimize your Google Business Profile Local Listing

  - ○ How to develop authority for your map listing via citation development

  - ○ List of the top citation sources for your business organization, according to the industry standards

  - ○ How to get real reviews from your customers in your true service area

    - ▪ Sample Review Card

    - ▪ Sample Review Request Email

    - ▪ Sample Review Us landing page for your website

- Understand Website Conversion Fundamentals - How to ensure that your website converts visitors into leads in the form of calls and web submissions

- Understand Mobile Optimization - How to optimize your website for mobile visitors

- Utilize Social Media Marketing - How to utilize Social Media (Facebook, Twitter, LinkedIn, and other social platforms for maximum effect in your business.

- Use Video Marketing - How to tap into the power of YouTube and other video sharing websites to enhance your visibility and drive better conversion

- Leverage email marketing tools (Constant Contact, Mail Chimp, etc.) to connect with your customers on a deeper level, receive more reviews, get more social media connections and ultimately get repeat and referral business.

- Understand and capitalize on Paid Online Advertising opportunities

- Use Pay-Per-Click Marketing (Google AdWords and Bing Search) - How to maximize the profitability of you Pay-Per-Click Marketing efforts

  ○ Why PPC should be part of your overall online marketing strategy

  ○ Why most PPC campaigns fail

  ○ Understanding the Google AdWords Auction process

  ○ How to configure and manage your Pay-Per-Clic campaign for maximum ROI

- Use Paid Online Directories - What paid online directories should you consider advertising in (A Place for Mom, Caring.com, BOTW, Spoke.com, Yahoo, Yelp, Foursquare, Yellowpages, etc.)

- Manage Pay-Per-Lead and Lead Services - How to properly manage Pay-Per-lead services for maximum return and long-term gains

  - Sample lead follow up email sequence

- Track, Measure and Quantify - How to track your online marketing plan to ensure your investment is generating a strong return

When it comes to Internet marketing for your business, there are several avenues to explore. In this chapter, we will briefly touch on the various Internet marketing channels that are available and then go into more detail throughout the book.

This chapter serves as your "Marketing Plan" and roadmap going forward.

Online Marketing Channels

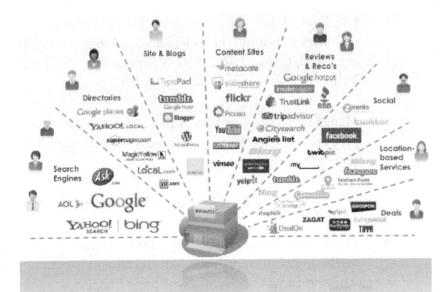

1. Search Engine Optimization (Organic Listings and Map Listings)
2. Search Engine Marketing/PPC on Google AdWords and Bing Search Network
3. Social Media Marketing (Facebook, Instagram, TikTok, Twitter, LinkedIn)
4. Video Marketing
5. Email Marketing
6. Free and Paid Directory Marketing (BOTW, Spoke.com, Yahoo, Yelp, Foursquare, Yellow Pages, etc…)
1. Paid Lead Services (A Place for Mom, Caring.com, Emfluence.com, Fuellead.com, Intellibright.com, etc…)

Search Engine Optimization

Search Engine Optimization (SEO) is the process of increasing your company's visibility on major search engines (Google, Yahoo, Bing, etc.) in the organic, non-paid listings as consumers are searching for your products or services. There are three very critical components of Search Engine Marketing. The three components are:

- Paid Listings – The area along the top and side that advertisers can bid on and pay for in order to obtain decent placement in the search engines

- Organic Listings – The area in the body of the Search Engine Results page

- Map Listings – These are the listings which come up beneath the paid listings and above the organic listings in a number of searches

Search Engine Optimization involves getting your website to show up in the Organic and Map Listings. These listings account for a majority of the search volume. As depicted in the illustration below, about 70% of searchers click on the Organic (non-paid listings) rather than the paid listings.

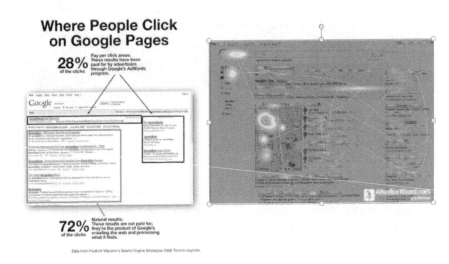

When most people think "Internet Marketing," they think Search Engine Optimization. However, you will begin to see that SEO is only a small piece of the MUCH BIGGER "Internet Marketing" puzzle for business owners.

Search Engine Marketing / Pay-Per-Click

Now that we have discussed SEO, let's talk about Search Engine Marketing or PPC (Pay-Per-Click). Google, Yahoo and Bing all have paid programs that allow you to BUY listings associated with your keywords to be placed in designated areas of their sites.

There are three really important benefits of PPC:

- Your keyword listings will appear on search engines almost immediately

- You only have to pay when someone actually clicks on your listing – hence the term Pay-Per-Click Marketing

- You can get your ad to show up on national terms in the areas/cities in which you operate

PPC Marketing works on an Auction system similar to that of eBay. You simply choose your keywords and propose a bid of what you would be willing to pay for each click.

There are several factors that determine placement which will be discussed in detail in the PPC for Businesses chapter. But, in the broadest sense, the one who is willing to pay the most per click will be rewarded the top position in the search engines, while the second-most will be in the second position, etc.

PPC Marketing is a great way to get your company's website to appear at the top of the search engines right away, driving qualified traffic to your website.

Social Media Marketing

You just can't deny Social Media's reach and influence (Facebook, TikTok, Twitter, Instagram, LinkedIn, YouTube), but how can it be utilized by an Assisted Living Facility which is just starting out? How can you use social media to grow your business? Just look at the staggering statistics for Facebook:

- More than 2.91 billion monthly active users (4th quarter 2021)

- 79% of monthly users log-on to Facebook on any given day

- Average user has 130 connections

- People spend over 700 billion minutes per month on Facebook

So, how can you employ this amazing tool to grow your business? Use it to connect with your personal sphere of influence, past and new customers. By doing so, you can solidify and maintain existing relationships, remain top-of-mind, and ultimately increase repeat and referral business.

Video Marketing

Did you know YouTube is the second-most used search engine on the market? Would you guess it is even ahead of Bing and Yahoo? It's true!

Millions of people conduct YouTube searches on a daily basis. Most business owners are so focused on SEO they completely neglect the opportunities that video and YouTube provide.

By implementing a Video Marketing Strategy for your business, you can get additional placement in search results for your keywords, enhance the effectiveness of your SEO efforts and improve visitor conversion.

Email Marketing

Similar to Social Media Marketing, email marketing is a great way to remain top-of-mind with your customers and increase repeat business and referrals. Compared to direct mail and newsletters, email marketing is by far the most cost-effective means to communicate with your customers.

As we will discuss in the Email Marketing for Businesses chapter, we feel email marketing can be used to effectively draw your customers into your social media world.

Paid Directory Marketing

There are a number of Online Directories that are important for businesses and specifically for Assisted Living Facilities:

1. BOTW (Businesses of the World)
2. AboutUs
3. Spoke
4. Yelp
5. Foursquare
6. YellowPages

Paid Lead Service Sites

There is an array of services that will sell you leads on a "pay-per-lead" basis or a flat monthly fee.

1. Emfluence
2. FuelLead
3. Intellibright

Specifically for Assisted Living Facilities the bigger players are:
4. A Place for Mom
5. Caring.com

While these leads tend to go to a number of different providers and will be less qualified than other sources, these Pay-Per-Lead services can be a profitable online marketing channel if executed correctly.

Now that you have an understanding of each of the Internet marketing channels available, in the following chapters, we will discuss how you can leverage them to connect with new customers and grow your business.

Where to Start?

With such a large amount of Internet marketing channels, where should you start? I firmly believe that over time, you should be appropriating each of these online marketing opportunities.

However, you must first begin with the foundation - your website, organic rankings, and social media/email. You should start looking at the various paid marketing opportunities when your website is set up correctly, ranking on search engines for your most important keywords in the organic, non-paid listings and you are actively engaging in social media activity.

We have found that the biggest and most impactful opportunity is getting ranked organically (in the non-paid listings). You may then leverage the additional profits in paid marketing to further augment your growth.

Once you are ranking well organically and things are firing on all cylinders, then you can start to run a well-managed Pay-Per-Click Campaign and explore paid online directory listings on Yelp, Foursquare, etc.

Next, let's look at the fundamentals of your overall marketing strategy before pressing forward into full implementation.

2 START WITH THE FUNDAMENTALS (MARKET, MESSAGE, MEDIA)

Before we delve into Internet Marketing, SEO, and Social Media Marketing, I want to be sure we have built a strong marketing foundation.

As I talk with various Assisted Living facilities across the United States, I have come to the realization the vast majority of you tend to skip straight past the basic fundamentals of your marketing strategy and dive headfirst into tactics (Pay-Per-Click adverting, SEO, Social Media, etc.).

So, what do I mean when I say "Fundamentals"? All marketing has 3 core components:

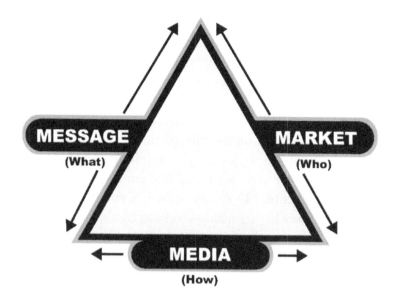

- Message (what)
- Market (who)
- Media (how)

You have to have a unique "Message" (who you are, what you do, what makes you unique, and why someone should hire you rather than another business offering the same service), a specifically defined "Market" (who you sell to and who your best customers are), and then look at "Media" (where you can reach those best customers). The tactics (Pay-Per-Click, SEO, Social Media, Direct Mail, etc.) fall into the "Media" category.

If you focus solely on the Media or Tactics, you will likely fail regardless of how well-selected that Media is. With that being said, you need to scale back to the fundamentals. Invest the time and energy in fleshing out your "Message" and figuring out who your "Market" is. By doing so, ALL of your Media choices will be vastly more effective. How can you do that?

Spend a few minutes and THINK. Take out a scratch pad

and answer these questions:

- How are you speaking with empathy and authority about your facility? Empathic messaging lets your potential guests know that you understand what they're experiencing in this stage of life. Authority shows families that you and your staff are competent to exceed their expectations when it comes to caring for them or their loved ones.

- What do I do which is unique and different from my competitors? (Do you offer a guaranteed time frame for your appointments? Do you offer written estimates prior to starting work, promising to stand by that estimate? Maybe you offer a guarantee for all of your work and will look after any issues within a one-year period of time after the project is complete. Perhaps you offer a free consultation to showcase the services you have to offer to potential customers.)

- If you think about the psychology of a customer, what concerns or apprehensions do you think they have about moving into an Assisted Living facility or their loved one moving in? "Will my Mom or Dad be well taken care of," or "Will there be enough activity to keep me engaged socially," or "How can I be sure my Dad's medical needs will be met?"

- How can you address your customers' common concerns in a unique way?

Market:

- Who is my ideal customer? (Please realize not everyone resides in your city nor within a 25-mile radius of your office) You need to be clear about the audience that you are looking to attract

- Look at your last 25 move-ins and evaluate who spend the most money, who had the highest profit margins, and who was genuinely pleased with your service. What are the unique characteristics of those good customers? Do they live in a particular area of town? Do they have a higher income level? How did they hear about your service offerings?

- Start to define who your ideal customer is so you can put a marketing plan in place to attract similar customers.

Once you have fleshed out your Message and your Market, then you can start to think about Media. In order to determine what media will be most effective for you, you need to think about where you can reach your IDEAL customer.

Clearly, the Internet is a great "media" for connecting with your ideal customer who is proactively in the market for your services. Throughout the remainder of this book, we will be explaining the various Internet marketing channels and how you can use them to connect with your ideal customer.

Remember, you need to start with the FUNDAMENTALS (Message, Market and Media) before running headstrong into any   marketing.

3 HOW TO SETUP YOUR WEBSITE

This chapter is all about how to setup your website. We are going to cover a lot of details as they relate to SEO, Google Maps Optimization, Pay-Per-Click Marketing, etc.

However, without a properly designed and functioning website, those efforts will be put to waste. Before you can or even should begin exploring those options, you must have your website up and running.

Formats

Let's talk about website formats and the different options available to you when you are ready to start.

1.   HTML Site – There are basic HTML pages and/or individual pages that can be incorporated into a website. This is how almost all websites were built several years ago. They had multiple pages hyper-linked together.

2.   Template Based Site Builders - Site builders, that you can obtain through providers such as GoDaddy, Wix, Squarespace are turnkey. You buy your domain and set up your website. I have found this type to be quite a bit less than ideal because you don't have a lot of controller flexibility, and

the overall experience isn't that great. But, there are still a lot of sites in this format. here.

3. CMS Systems - Content Management Systems, like WordPress, Webflow, Duda, Joomla, Drupal. I'm sure there are many others but these are the big ones.

Given my experience with websites, a content management system (CMS) is ideal for a business. I say that because you have scalability. In any of these platforms, you have the ability to change your navigation on the fly, add as many pages as you need, and easily scale out your site.

If you have your website built in HTML format with graphics behind the website, and you wanted to add a new section, you would have to start from scratch.

You would have to go back to the graphics and modify all of the pages in order to add the new section to your navigational structure. You'd basically be using technology that is old and outdated. With a CMS, everything is built behind code allowing the ability to apply easy edits and to add multiple pages.

As you will see in the search engine optimization section of the book, you will have the ability to have a page for each one of your services and each city in which you operate.

A CMS allows you to create your pages in a scalable format without having to mess around with the graphics or do anything that is difficult to control. Also, it is easy to access, modify, and update.

Using formats like WordPress and Joomla, you may access the back-end administrative area at yourcompany.com/login.

After entering your username and password, you will find there is a very easy to edit system with pages and posts which function similarly to Microsoft Word.

You can input text, import images and press "save", forcing all new edits to be updated on your live website. It is easier than it looks and is very search engine friendly.

Content Management Systems have intelligently structured linking between pages and content, making it extremely search engine friendly. We have found this method tends to be better than regular HTML or other options.

In a lot of cases, a blog is going to be automatically bolted onto a CMS based website providing you with a section where you may feed updates. In the SEO chapter, we cover the importance of creating consistent updates and blogging regularly.

Another benefit of content management systems is being provided with a variety of plugins you can choose to incorporate on your website. You can easily pull in your social media feeds, YouTube Videos, and check-ins.

You may also syndicate your website to automatically post any new updates to your social media profiles. You can add map integration where people can click to either get instructions or view a map to find out the areas which are served by your organization. There is a surplus of features available within a CMS that you can't necessarily do with a non-CMS type option.

Whether you are looking to build a website from the ground

up, you are just getting started, or you feel like you simply need a redesign, I highly suggest that you do so in CMS, ideally in WordPress.

WordPress is a fantastic platform and very easy to use. It's the most adopted website platform available with many developers using it. It's constantly being updated and improved and I have found it to work very well for different businesses.

You have my stamp of approval to go out and build your website on a WordPress platform.

What Should Your Website Include?

So, what pages should your website have? What navigation structure should you create? Depending on your business, you will need to showcase different things. For most businesses though, the basics should be:

1. Home
2. About Us
3. Our Services
4. Location (This will make more sense when you read the SEO Chapter)
5. Reviews and Testimonials
6. Blog
7. Contact Us

These are the core pages. Within "About Us," you might incorporate a drop-down menu for subcategories including "Meet the Staff," "Why Choose Our Company," etc. I think that's very powerful.

You want to be able to drive people back to a "Why Choose Us" section, and, in some cases, if you are having issues recruiting and retaining good quality talent, you might want to have a "Careers" page under the "About Us" navigation, where a visitor can go and fill out an application and learn more about your organization.

Within "Our Services," you want to have the ability to list a drop-down listing the types of services that you offer. We discuss this to a great extent in the SEO chapter.

You want to have landing pages for each one of your services because they are going to be optimized with different keyword combinations.

A "Reviews and Testimonials" page will provide a section to showcase what your customers are saying about you in text or video form.

You can also pull in reviews from sites such as Google Business Profile, Angie's List, and Yelp. Finally, of course, you will need a "Contact Us" page where web visitors have your general contact information, driving directions, and map.

These are the core things you should have on your website.

A Clear Description of Who You Are

We call this "passing the grunt test". If a caveman stumbled upon your website would he know exactly how you are helping seniors live a better life and in what area?

This means it's important to clearly mention your business name and sum up your products or services above the fold section of your website. A clear and specific description will attract the visitor's attention immediately - within two to three seconds - and encourage them to spend time on your website.

Your Primary Contact Details

Outside of your navigational structure, what else should your website have? What other elements are going to help with conversion?

Well, you should always provide a primary phone number on every page of your website, in the upper right-hand corner. When somebody visits a page, their eyes are naturally drawn to the top section of the website where they can see the logo and the phone number.

People tend to expect that phone number will be somewhere in this location. It is ideal to have a prominent phone number, telling them to "call you now" for service in that section.

An Obvious and Consistent Call to Action

I believe business websites should always make a web form available from which a customer can easily book a tour of your facility. Bear in mind that every visitor to your website is in a different situation and frame of mind. You may have someone that's on their phone or just leisurely looking to contact you for more information and is able to simply pick up the phone and call you.

On the other hand, somebody who's in a work environment may not have the ability to stop what they are doing and make a phone call without drawing attention from his or her coworkers. However, they may be able to browse around online to find out what options are available.

Your potential customers may reach your website and be torn between making a call right at that moment, just scheduling the appointment, or wanting to have someone from your team contact them.

Make it easy for them to enter their information into a web form where they can provide their name, phone number, email address, and a note detailing their requests that they can send through online. It makes it easier and doesn't create any pressure.

The Ability to Chat or Two-Way Text You

Not everyone is going to want to call or book a tour of your home. Many Assisted Living facilities are now offering the ability to chat directly with website visitors as well as request a text. If you're not doing this I can almost guarantee you that you are missing out on new tours and move-ins. If you have a CMS-style website like I mentioned earlier this is an easy add-on for your web team.

Social Media Links

You also want to provide links to your social media profiles. Link to Facebook, Instagram, Twitter, and LinkedIn so customers can easily jump off, engage with you on social media, see what you're doing and be able to press that important "like," "follow" or "subscribe" button. It helps create a sense of authenticity when your customers get to see your social media content.

Customer Testimonials

Have a direct link that drives visitors to your online reviews and testimonials that we discussed previously.

You should also post your credentials either in the sidebar or in the header graphic, proving, for example, that you're BBB-accredited or a member of the local chamber of commerce or industry association.

This allows potential customers to rest assured that you are a credible organization, you're involved in the community, and that you're less apt to provide them with poor service. They'll feel more comfortable doing business with you.

You definitely need to have your company name, address, and phone number on every page of your website.

It is not critical that you list your address on each page because it will not be a determining factor in whether or not customers call you, but as I will explain in the Google Business Profile optimization chapter, having name, address and phone number consistency is critical for ranking on Google Business Profile.

It is a great strategy to have your name, address, and phone number referenced on your website, ideally in the footer section. You need to have that contact information on all of your pages including the Contact Us page, of course.

Authentic Images

It's extremely important that you infuse personality into your website. By personality, I'm referring to authentic photos and videos.

Showcase your facility, feature yourself, the business owner, and the people who work in the business: the staff, caregivers, etc.

Showcase the facility itself, the common areas, and outside areas if you have them. Don't use stock photography, but authentic imagery. This gives the visitor the chance to get to know, like, and trust you, before they even pick up the phone. I've seen this tactic prove itself time and time again.

Say a potential guest visited two different facilities and is making their final choice on where to move in. One of them is generic and is obviously using stock photography.

The other website highlights a genuine picture of the actual facility, the team, and social areas. This authentic page converts 10 to 1. You must let your real personality reflect on the website.

You must also craft clear messaging that explains why they should choose your assisted living facility. Why should someone choose you over the competition?

Pull them down a path where they can start to learn more about why you are their best option. Where they can see your online reviews, and if they're kind of on the fence, where they can quickly locate some special offers and incentives that will drive action. This will get them to contact you right away, as opposed to continuing to browse the web for someone else.

Mobile Website

The other major thing you want to think about, from the conversion perspective, is having a mobile-ready version of your website.

At least 50% of your web visitors are accessing the Internet via smart phones such as iPhones and Android phones. Make sure the mobile version of your site isn't the same as your regular site.

It should be condensed, fitting their screen and giving them just the information that they need. It should integrate with their phone so all they have to do is press a button to call you.

People who are searching or accessing your website from a mobile device are in a different state of mind than the people that are browsing and finding you on a computer. Make it easy

for them to get the information they need and to get in touch
with you.

Use an easy "click to call" button that is easy to see and
access.

4 UNDERSTANDING HOW SEARCH ENGINES WORK AND THE DIFFERENCES BETWEEN THE PAID, ORGANIC, AND MAP LISTINGS

In this section, we want to take a few minutes to demystify the search engines and break down the anatomy of the Search Engine Results Page. By understanding how each component works, you can formulate a strategy to maximize your results.

There are three core components of the Search Engines Results   page:

1. Paid/PPC Listings
4. Map Listings
5. Organic Listings

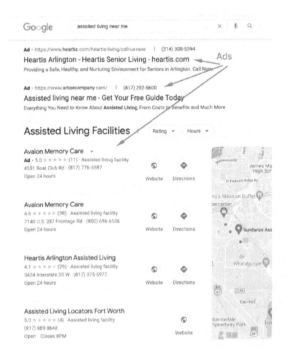

1. **Paid/PPC Listings** – In the paid section of the search engines you can select keywords that are relevant to Assisted Living, and then pay to be listed amongst the search results. The reason it is referred to as PPC or Pay-Per-Click1 is that rather than paying a flat monthly or daily fee for placement, you simply pay each time someone clicks on the link.

2. **Map Listings** – The map listings have become very important because they are the first thing that comes up in search results for most locally based searches. If someone searches for some particular service in your area, chances are the map listings will be the first thing they look at. Unlike the paid section of the search engine, you can't buy your way into the Map Listings. You must earn it. Once you do, there is no

per-click cost associated with being in this section of the search engine.

3. **Organic Listings** – The organic/natural section of the Search Engine Results page appears directly beneath the Map Listings in many local searches but appears directly beneath the Paid Listings in the absence of the Map Listings (the Map Section only shows up in specific local searches). Similar to the Map Listings, you can't pay your way into this section of the search engines and there is no per-click cost associated with it.

Now that you understand the three major components of the Search Engine Results and the differences between Paid Listings, Map Listings, and Organic Listings you might wonder... "What section is the most important?"

This is a question that we receive from a large number of businesses every day.

The fact is all three components are important, and each should have a place in your online marketing program because you want to show up as often as possible when someone is searching for your service offerings in your area.

Return On Investment

With that said, assuming you are operating on a limited budget and need to make each marketing dollar count, you need to focus your investment on the sections that are going to drive the strongest Return On Investment(ROI).

Research indicates that the vast majority of the population looks directly at the Organic and Map Listings when conducting a search, and their eyes simply glance over the Paid Listings (as illustrated by the images below).

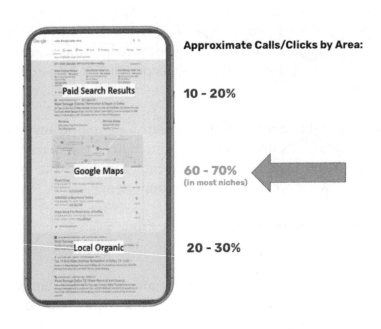

Approximate Calls/Clicks by Area:

Paid Search Results — **10 - 20%**

Google Maps — **60 - 70%** (in most niches)

Local Organic — **20 - 30%**

So, if you are operating on a limited budget and need to get the best bang for your buck, start by focusing your efforts on the area which gets the most clicks at the lowest cost. We have found placement in the Organic and Map section on the Search Engines drive a SIGNIFICANTLY higher Return On Investment than Pay-Per-Click Marketing.

However, ranking organically in the Map section or on page one of the organic results can take some time. I like to tell clients they should expect 5 months on the low end and up to 12 months on the high end. In an industry like Senior Housing, the competition in your area could be really high in highly populated areas and a little less competitive in lower population areas.

We advise clients to immediately start working on organic SEO, and start a lower budget PPC campaign to get some early wins.

In the next chapter, we will start to look at Search Engine Optimization and how to optimize your website to rank in the organic listings (non-paid) for the most important keywords in your field.

How Do Search Engines Work?

It is also important to understand how search engines work. This includes the process of crawling and indexing, plus the concept of page rank as well.

Search engines work by crawling billions of web pages using their own web crawlers or web spiders. These web crawlers are also known as Search engine bots.

Understanding Search Engine Index
Once a webpage is discovered by a search engine, they are added into a search engine data structure which is called index. Search engine index includes all the crawled web URLs along with several important key elements about the content of each web URL such as:

- The keywords
- Type of content
- Uniqueness of the page
- User engagement with the page

Understanding Search Engine Algorithm

Search engine algorithm aims to display a relevant set of high-quality search results that will fulfill the user's search query as quickly as possible.

What Happens When a Search Query is Entered?

When a search query is entered into the search engine by a potential user, the search engine tries to identify all the pages which are deemed relevant.

During this process, the search engine uses a special algorithm to hierarchically rank the most relevant pages into a set of results. The algorithm which is used to rank the most relevant web pages differs for each search engine.

For example, a web page that ranks on the top for a search query in Google may not rank highly for the same query in Bing.

Mentioned below are a few elements search engines use to return the results.

- Search query
- Location
- Previous search history
- Device from which the search query was entered

Sources and References:
https://en.wikipedia.org/wiki/Pay-per-click

https://en.wikipedia.org/wiki/Web_crawler

5 SEARCH ENGINE OPTIMIZATION - HOW TO OPTIMIZE YOUR WEBSITE FOR THE KEYWORDS THAT ARE MOST IMPORTANT FOR YOUR PARTICULAR BUSINESS

Getting your company listed in the organic section (non-paid listings) of the search engines comes down to two core factors:

• Having the proper on-page optimization so Google knows what you do and the general area you serve. This allows it to put in the index for the right keywords. You do this by having pages for each of your services and then optimizing them for specific keyword combinations (Ex. Your City + main service, Your City + service 2, Your City + service 3, etc.).

• Creating enough authority and transparency so Google ranks you on page one (rather than page ten) for those specific keywords. Ultimately, it comes down to having credible inbound links and citations from other websites to your website and its sub-pages. He who has the most credible inbound links, citations, and reviews will be the most successful.

Throughout the course of this chapter, I provide specific how-to information on exactly what pages to add to your business website - and why. I also discuss what you can do to improve your authority/transparency in Google's eyes so your website ranks on page one for the keywords which are most important to your business.

Before you start creating pages and trying to do the "on-page optimization" work, you need to be clear on the most commonly searched keywords relative to the services you offer.

By understanding the keywords, you can be sure to optimize your website for the words that will actually drive qualified traffic to your site. One needs to conduct detailed research of the market and the requirements that potential customers have in order to find the optimal keywords which will help you bring in more customers.

Given that different organizations might be working in different industries, it is imperative businesses learn the methodology behind selecting the most relevant keywords for their services. We have provided an overview of how to conduct keyword research.

How to Conduct Keyword Research

To determine what your customers are searching for when they need your services, here are a number of tools that can be used to conduct keyword research. Some are free of charge while others have a monthly cost associated with them. Some of the better keyword research tools include Wordstream, Google AdWords Keyword Tool and SEM Rush.

For the purposes of this book, we have developed instructions based on the free Google AdWords Keyword tool. To use Google AdWords Keyword tool, you'll need to:

- Develop a list of your services and save it in a .txt file
- Develop a list of the cities that you operate in (your

primary city of service and the smaller surrounding towns) and save it in a .txt file

- Go to www.mergewords.com

Now that you're at merge words, you'll want to follow this click path. 1) Paste your list of cities in column one 2) Paste your list of services in column two 3) Press the "Merge!" button.

The tool will generate a list of all your services combined with your cites of service.

- Go to Google.com and search "Google Keyword Tool" or go directly to https://adwords.google.com/o/KeywordTool

Now that you're inside the adwords tool, paste your list of merged keywords into the "word or phrase" box and press submit.

- You will now see a list of each of your keywords with a "search volume" number beside it

- Sort the list from greatest to smallest

You now have a list of the most commonly searched keywords in your area.

With this list, you can map out keywords to specific pages on your website and rest assured that you are basing your strategy on opportunity rather than a guesstimate.

Most Commonly Searched Industry Keywords

Below you will find the list of the most commonly search keywords for the Assisted Living space.

| assisted living near me | 135,000 |
| senior living near me | 60,500 |

assisted living facilities near me	27,100
senior communities near me	6,600
senior homes near me	4,400
senior home near me	4,400
senior living community near me	3,600
senior care near me	3,600
senior assisted living near me	2,900
assisted living homes near me	1,900
assisted living home near me	1,900
memory care near me	790

Based on this data, in order to get the most from the Internet from an SEO perspective, you will want to create content on your website for the following keyword combinations that would make sense for your area. The example below is for Philadelphia, PA. This table is showing keywords for the category of Assisted Living and Memory Care. You could do the exact same thing for other categories like: Senior Living, Independent Living Home, Assisted Living Facilities and so on.

Assisted Living	Memory Care

Assisted Living	Memory Care
Philadelphia assisted living	Philadelphia memory care
Philadelphia PA assisted living	Philadelphia PA memory care
Philadelphia Pennsylvania assisted living	Philadelphia Pennsylvania memory care
assisted living Philadelphia	memory care Philadelphia
assisted living Philadelphia PA	memory care Philadelphia PA
assisted living Philadelphia Pennsylvania	memory care Philadelphia Pennsylvania
assisted living in Philadelphia	memory care in Philadelphia
assisted living in Philadelphia PA	memory care in Philadelphia PA
assisted living in Philadelphia Pennsylvania	memory care in Philadelphia Pennsylvania
assisted living near Philadelphia	memory care near Philadelphia
assisted living near Philadelphia PA	memory care near Philadelphia PA
assisted living near Philadelphia Pennsylvania	memory care near Philadelphia Pennsylvania
assisted living near me	memory care near me

How to Map Out Your Website Pages for Maximum Result

Now that you are set to determine the most commonly searched keywords in your field, you can begin mapping out the pages which need to be added to your website.

Keep in mind each page on your website can only be optimized for 1-2 keyword combinations. If you came up with 25 keywords, then you are going to need at least 12 – 15 landing pages.

Be sure you have each keyword mapped to a specific page on your site.

Keyword	Mapped to What Page
Main Keyword	Home
Keyword 1	Services - Keyword 1
Keyword 2	Services - Keyword 2
Keyword 3	Services - Keyword 3
Keyword 4	Services - Keyword 4
Keyword 5	Services - Keyword 5

Here is an example for an Assisted Living Facility that has the following keywords: assisted living facility, senior living community, memory care, independent living, adult day care

Keyword	Mapped to What Page
assisted living facility	Home
Senior living community	Home
Memory Care	Memory Care Page
Independent Living	Independent Living Page
Adult Day Care	Adult Day Care Page

Now that you have mapped out the pages to be included on your website, you can start thinking about how to optimize each of those pages for the major search engines (Google, Bing, Duck Duck Go, Neeva).

How to Optimize for Ranking in the Organic Listings

Step 1 – Build the website and obtain more placeholders on the major search engines.

A typical services website has only 5-6 pages (Home – About Us – Our Services – Testimonials - Contact Us).

That does not create a lot of indexation or placeholders on the major search engines. Most ALFs, for example, provide a wide variety of services, as covered in the Keyword Research section of this chapter.

By building out the website and creating separate pages highlighting each of these services offered (combined with city modifiers), a business can get listed on the search engines for each of those different keyword combinations.

Here is an example:
Home   –   About   –   Coupons   –   Contact   Us

Sub-pages for each service – Dallas Assisted Living, Dallas Memory Care, Dallas Adult Day Care, Dallas Independent Living,   Dallas   Senior   Living   Community

Assisted Living Facilities often provide services in a large number of locations outside of their primary city. In order to be found on the major search engines for EACH of those sub-cities, additional pages need to be created:

• Sub-pages for each sub-city serviced - Assisted Living, Memory Care, Independent Living, etc.

Step 2 – Optimize Pages for Search Engines:

Once the pages and sub-pages are built for each of your core services, each page needs to be optimized from an SEO perspective in order to make the search engines understand what the page is about.

Here are some of the most important items that need to be taken care of for on-page search engine optimization:

- Unique Title Tag on each page
- H1 Tag restating that Title Tag on each page
- Images named with primary keywords (alt text)
- URL containing page keyword
- Anchor Text on each page and built into Footer – Dallas Assisted Living Facility
- XML Sitemap should be created and submitted to Google Webmaster Tools and Bing Webmaster Tools

How to Build Up Website Authority

Once the pages are built and the "on-page" SEO is complete, the next step is getting inbound links so you can rank on page one for your most important keywords.

Everything we have discussed to this point is sort of like laying the groundwork. The pages need to be in order to even be in the running. However, it is the number of QUALITY inbound links and web references to those pages that is going to determine placement.

30% of SEO is On-Page type work
The other 70% is Link Building

Building the pages is just the beginning. The only way to get your site to rank above your competition is by having MORE quality inbound links and citations to your site.

Again, if there is any secret sauce to ranking well in the

search engines, it really is links and authority. The major caveat? You can't just use garbage links. You don't want to just have a thousand links. When I say links, I'm referring to other websites hyper-linking to your website, which I'll explain a little bit more with specific examples.

Some of the latest algorithm changes (Google Panda and Google Penguin) involve Google trying to prevent spam. A lot of Internet marketers and SEO coordinators realize it's all about the links. That is what the Google algorithm was built upon. They figured out ways to get a variety of links with random anchor text pointed back to the pages that they want to have ranked. Google has recognized that if those links are not relevant, then they don't add any value to the Internet.

Bad or irrelevant links can actually hurt your ranking more than help it. It's about getting quality, relevant links back to your home page and subpages through content creation and strategic link-building. How do you get the links? Where do you get the links?

Take a look at the list below as a point of reference.

1. Association Links – Be sure that you have a link to your site from any industry associations that you belong to (Ex. Business associations, Chamber of Commerce, Networking Groups, etc.).

2. Directory Listings – Get your site listed on as many directory type websites as possible (Angie's List, Yahoo Local Directory, Judy's Book, Yelp.com, etc.)

3. Create Interesting Content/Articles - This is probably the #1 source of inbound links. For example, you can write an article about a particular service offering in your industry and push it out to thousands of people through article

45

directory sites that may each contain a link back to a specific page on your site.

4. Competitive Link Acquisition – This is the process of using tools like Raven Tools, SEO Book and others to see what links your top competitors have, and then get those same or similar links pointed back to your website.

5. Local Links - ALFs are local and that means you need links from local organizations. Here you need to be thinking about private schools, churches, sports associations. This can be an easy opportunity to capitalize on the things you're already doing in the community. See if they sponsorships available or of they would be interested in something like this if they don't already have a program.

Directory Links - There's a number of what I like to call "low-hanging fruit" links.

It all starts with your online directory listings.

Some examples include Google Business Profile, City Search, Yelp.com, Judy's Book, Best of the Web, Yellow Pages, Hot Frog, Assisted Living Directory, and the list goes on. All of those online listings let you display your company name, address, phone number and a link back to your website. Some of them even allow reviews.

For the most part, adding your business information to those directories is completely free of charge. You want to make sure that you have your company listed on as many of the online directory listings as possible for authoritative linking reasons.

They're also valuable from the Google Maps optimization perspective because they give you citations which are very important for getting ranked on the map.

A great way to find additional online directories to add your company to would be to run a search in Google for "Assisted Living Facility – Business Directory" or "Your City – Business Directory". This will give you a great list of potential directory sites to add your company to.

There are also tools for this like BrightLocal or White Spark that can provide you with a list of directory sources based on your industry. After beginning with online directory listings, you want to look at any associations you're involved with.

Association Links – I'm assuming you are involved in some type of association, whether it is the national industry association, the local chapter or some other group affiliation.

Visit the websites of those organizations and get listed in the member section. This will give you citations and the opportunity to link back to your website.

Non-Competitive Affiliated Industries and Local Businesses - You can work with colleagues that have affiliated industry type businesses.

Supplier Sites – Look at the suppliers you purchase from and try to coordinate a deal with them. Oftentimes, the places where you buy your merchandise will have a section on their website that mentions their value add resellers. You can get a link from those.

Social Media Profile Links - The other "low-hanging fruit" links are social media profiles. We have a whole chapter about the power of social media and how you can harness it to get repeat and referral business.

Simply from a link-building perspective, you should set up a

Facebook page, Twitter account, LinkedIn profile, Pinterest profile and a YouTube channel and place a link to your website on each.

All of them will allow you to enter your company's name, address, phone number, a description and, of course, a place to put your website address.

Local Association - Other local associations that you're involved in. If you're a member of the Chamber of Commerce, a networking group like BNI (Business Networking International), or if you're involved with a local charity, find out if they list their members on their websites. Another great place to get links is by typing in your city directory.

Competitive Link Acquisition - You might be surprised that if you really tackle these elements and you don't do any of the other things we have discussed, you will notice that you've probably got enough links to outrank your competition in your area.

I want to share some additional thoughts and strategies on how you can accomplish even more from a link building perspective. A very powerful strategy that you can implement is called Competitive Link Acquisition.

The way I like to think of it is that if quantity inbound links are the secret sauce to outranking your competition, and if we could figure out who's linking to your competition or what links your competition have, and we can get those same or similar links pointed back to your website, then you can outrank them because you'll at that point have more authority.

Competitive link acquisition is the process of figuring out who is in the top position for your most important keywords reverse engineering their link profile to see what links they have, and getting those same or similar links pointed back to your website. A simple way to do this is just to go to Google.com and type in "your city + your service," and find out who is in the top few positions.

Let's take a look at the number one placeholder. He's there because his website is optimized well and Google knows he should be ranked well based on the quality and quantity inbound links compared to the competition.

Once you know who he is, you can use a couple of different tools such as Raven Tools, Majestic SEO, Back Link Watch, etc., and you can take their URL, input it into your tool of choice, run the report, and get a list of links in return.

So, your number one competitor is competitor.com. Your tool spits out a list showing they have 392 inbound links.

- He's got a link from the local Chamber of Commerce
- He's got a link from the PHCC
- He's got a link from an article that he posted in the local newspaper
- He's got a link from the local networking chapter

By analyzing the types of links he has, you can systematically mimic those links and get them pointed back to your website.

Don't just do this for your first competitor, but also for your second and third and fourth and fifth competitors. By doing this on a consistent basis, you can start to dominate the search engines for your most important keywords.

If you build out your site for your services and sub-services, optimize the pages using SEO best practices and then systematically obtain inbound links, you will start to DOMINATE the search engines for your service-related keywords in your area.

Content Marketing Strategies for Maintaining Relevance

Another highly important factor in SEO is maintaining relevance in your market by adding ongoing relevant updates to your website. It is still true that content is king.

Google Loves Fresh Content!

In some cases, with the changes in the algorithm, just because you've got a great website with the right title tags and all the best links, you may get discounted if they're not seeing fresh information posted on a consistent basis.

Google loves fresh content, and it is important to have a methodology where you are creating and posting content to your website on a regular basis. I want to give you a framework for figuring out what kind of content you could write, why you should create content, and how you can do it consistently.

First, you need to understand and accept that you need to become a subject matter expert. You might not consider yourself a writer or a content creator, but you are a subject matter expert.

There are things you know that the general population does not. You're an expert when it comes to the service you are offering, and you have a team of people who are proficient in this area as well. You can create content on the topic that you know most about.

You can write about a variety of different topics including 1-2 relevant keywords with the same. You may not think it at first, but there are a lot of different topics in your industry you can come up with to create content about.

Types of Content

You should also consider that content doesn't have to be just written words. It's doesn't have to be just articles. Content can come in a variety of forms. The most popular are going to be articles, photos, videos and audio files. Stop and think about what content creation method works best for you.

Some people are great writers and that's their strength. Other people like to be on camera. I personally like to create videos. I'm very comfortable creating videos. Other people can talk (and they can talk your ear off about whatever topic they are passionate about!)

You can create content in many different ways. Because it is what I enjoy, I'll use video as an example. A business director can set up a camera and record himself explaining the services his company has to offer in the market, in the same manner that he would explain it to a customer.

Now you'll actually have multiple pieces of content. You'll have a video, which can be uploaded to YouTube, Vimeo, Meta Café, etc. This one piece of content can create multiple invaluable links to your website.

You can also take that video, save the audio portion of it, and you've got an audio clip. You can upload that audio file to your website and post on other various sites.

You can use a transcription service like Rev or Descript, for instance, where you upload the audio or video file and somebody converts it to text or they'll use AI for an even cheaper price.

For a couple of bucks, you'll have a complete article comprised of what you said. Now you've got a piece of content you can post to your blog. You can put it on eHow or one of those other article directory sites.

Content Consistency

You want to create content on a consistent basis, using the blog on your website as the hub to post it, but then syndicating it to various sources.

Syndicating it to article directory sites if it's in text form, and sending it to video sites like Vimeo, Metacafe and YouTube.com if it's in video form. Doing this keeps the content fresh on your website/domain and creates a lot of authority, which is really going to help with the overall ranking of the website on the search engines.

You want to make sure you're appropriating each one of

these link-building opportunities to maximize your rank-potential in your area. You might be surprised that the services you offer are highly competitive from a SEO perspective. There are a lot of companies who want to rank for the same keywords, and many of them have invested heavily in the Internet and in getting themselves higher in the search engines.

Now that you've built out your website, you've optimized it correctly, and you've got an ongoing link-building and content development strategy in place, you want to start looking at Google Business Profile Optimization. and getting ranked on the Google Map Pack.

6 GOOGLE BUSINESS PROFILE OPTIMIZATION - HOW TO GET RANKED IN THE MAP 3 PACK

The Fundamentals of Google Maps Ranking (NAP, Citations, Consistency and Reviews)

Getting listed on the first page of Google for "Your City + Service" comes down to five primary factors:

- Having a claimed and verified Google Business Profile
- Having an optimized Google Business Profile listing for the area you operate in
- Having a consistent N.A.P. (Name, Address, Phone Number Profile) across the web so that Google feels confident that you are a legitimate organization located in the place you have listed and serving the market you claim to serve.
- Having reviews from your customers in your service area
- Local Links from business and organizations that in proximity to your business

If you have each of these four factors working in your favo you will SIGNIFICANTLY improve the probability of ranking on page one of Google Maps in your market.

How to establish a strong Name, Address, Phone Numbe

profile

As I mentioned above, having a consistent Name, Address, Phone Number Profile across the web is essential for ranking well on Google Map Pack in your area. Google sees it as a signal of authority.

Rather than jumping directly into claiming your Google Business Profile listing and citation-building, it's critical that you start by determining your true N.A.P. so that you can ensure that it is referenced consistently across the web.

When I say making sure it's consistent, you want to be certain that you are always referencing the legitimate name for your business.

If your company's name is "Sharron's Care Facility", you must always list it as "Sharron's Care Facility," as opposed to just "Sharron's Care."

The other thing you should be aware of is that there is a lot of misinformation about how to list your company name online. You may read information suggesting that you keyword your name.

For example, if your name is "Sharron's Care Facility," somebody might tell you it would be really smart if you just added to the title of your company "Sharron's Business | Dallas Business," for instance.

While that may have worked back in the day, it's no longer an effective strategy. It's actually a violation of Google's policies and procedures.

Make sure you list your exact company name the same way across the board on all your directory sources. Also make sure that you use the same phone number in all those places. I'm a big advocate for tracking phone numbers and what is happening with your marketing. But, when it comes to your online directory listings, you want to use your primary business phone number that you've been using from the beginning.

Don't try to create some unique number for each one of your directories. What that does is confuse your name/address profile. It will hurt you.

Use your primary phone number in all those places, use your exact company name, and use your principal address, written the same way. If your business is located at "1367 South West 87th Street, Suite Number 105, " make sure you list it just like that every single time. Even minor changes such as "STE 105" will affect your Google Business.

Don't Forget the Little Details!

Don't neglect to include the suite in one place and then put it on in another. Don't spell out "South West" in one place and put "SW" in the other. Even putting "STE" instead of "Suite" will have a negative effect. We are driving for a consistent name/address profile across the web.

A good way to figure out what Google considers to be your N.A.P. is to run a search on Google for "Your Company" and see what is being referenced on the Google Map.

See how that compares to the other high authority sites like YP.com, Yelp.com, Angie's List and others. Look for the predominant combination of N.A.P. and reference that for all your directory work going forward.

How to Properly Claim and Optimize Your Google Business Profile Listing

Below you will find a step-by-step guide for checking, claiming and managing your Local Business Listings on Google.

1. Go to https://google.com/business
6. Create an Account and claim your business

7. Enter your business address and all pertinent information. Remember, your Name, Address, and Phone number should be consistent across the internet.

8. Choose a verification method - This is evolving because Google is doing it's best to weed out any spam accounts. We've seen them even do some live video verification where the business owner needs to be on a live video call and show their face and their place of business.

9. Once you've created a profile, go to your Google Business Profile Dashboard and fill in all the necessary information to optimize your profile. Set aside a good block of time for this. You need to fill out the profile as completely as you can.

• Update Your Company Name to Read "Company Name") – e.g. Sharron's Home. Don't add any additional keywords
                                                                              here

• Add your Website Address – This will create an important   inbound   link

• Upload PHOTOS – AS MANY AS POSSIBLE – Use personal photos, pictures of yourself (the owner), your staff, the facilities, your bedrooms, activities, the company logo, coupons, and your lots of smiling faces. People Connect and Resonate with images. Leverage that in your Map Listing

- Upload a video if you have one (If you don't – Get one made!)

- List your hours of operation and services offered

Optimize your Google Business Profile

You'll manage your business listing from your Google Business Profile Dashboard.

Here's where you'll make changes to your company information, gain insights into how popular your business is by seeing how many times your profile has been viewed on Google Maps.

There are a number of Best Practices you need to be aware of to properly optimize your Map listing.

Company Name – Always use your legal Company Name – don't cram additional words into the name field. Ex. If your company name is "Evergreen Homes," don't try to put additional keywords like "Evergreen Homes – Dallas". This would be against Google's guidelines and will reduce your probability of ranking.

Address – On the "Address Field" use your EXACT legal address. You want to ensure that you have the same address listed on your Google listing as it is on all the other online directory listings like YellowPages.com, CitySearch.com, Yelp.com, etc. The consistency of your N.A.P. (Name, Address, Phone Number Profile) is very important for placement.

Phone Number – Use a local number (not an 800 number), and make sure it is your real office number rather than a tracking number. We find that 800 numbers don't rank well. If you use a tracking number, it won't be consistent with your other online directory listings and will result in poor ranking.

Categories – We suggest you use three categories and now more. Be sure to use categories that describe what your business "is" rather than what it "does". So, you can use "Assisted Living Facility" "Senior Care Communities" etc. rather than "Nursing Assistance" or "Meals Provided." The latter would be considered a violation of Google's regulations and would hurt rather than help you.

Service Area and Location Settings – Google offers two options here:

No, all customers come to my location
Yes, I serve customers at their location

For any Assisted Living Facility or Home with a physical location that you serve your customers at, you would select "No."

If your business is a placement service or any other vendor serving the Assisted Living industry, you would select "Yes" if you are an online service provider OR travel to your customer's locations to provide a service.

"Do not show my address". If you work from a home office, it is required that you select "Do not show my address." Google is really working to create a great user experience, and if you have a business listed at your home address or your Aunt Sally's address, but you don't serve customers there, you'll eventually get filtered out of the results. It's not worth trying to game Google.

Picture and Video Settings – You can upload up to ten pictures and five videos. Use this opportunity to upload authentic content about your company. It's always best to use real photos of your team, facilities, and activities rather than stock photos.

Pictures – You can get more juice from this section by saving the images to your hard drive with a naming convention like "your city + Assisted Living – your company name," rather than the standard file name. You can also create geo context for the photos by using a service like Geotag.Online or GeoImgr.com

Videos – Upload VIDEOS. They don't have to be professionally produced and will resonate well with your customers. A best practice is to upload the videos to YouTube and then Geo Tag them using the advanced settings.

Once you have optimized your listing using the best practices referenced above, you want to be sure that you don't have any duplicate listings on Google Maps.

Duplicate Listings

We have found that even just one or two duplicates can prevent your listing from ranking on page one. In order to identify and merge duplicate listings, run a search on Google for "Company Name, City".

To clean up duplicates, click on the listing in question and then click "edit business details."

Click "This is a duplicate" to let Google know that the listing should be merged with your primary listing.

If you follow these best practices, you will have a well optimized Google Maps listing for your Business.

How to Develop Authority for your Map Listing via Citation Development

Now that you have claimed your Google Business Profile listing and optimized it to its fullest, you need to build authority.

Having a well-claimed and optimized local listing doesn't automatically rank you on page one. Google wants to list the most legitimate and qualified providers first. So, how do they figure out who gets the page one listings?

Well, there are a number of determining factors, but one of them is how widely the company is referenced on various online directory sites such as Yellow Pages, City Search, Yelp and others.

Citations are web references to your company name, address and phone number. You can add citations in a variety of ways. There are directory listings that you should claim manually and others that you can submit to via submission services like Universal Business Listing or Yext.com.

My personal preference is to claim listings manually, ensuring that I am in control and can make updates/edits as needed.

Top Citation Sources to Claim Manually

- Google Business Profile
- Bing Local
- Yahoo Local
- City Search
- FourSquare
- Yelp
- YP
- Merchant Circle
- Manta

List of the Top Citation Sources for Businesses

1. Google - Google is probably the most important and most talked-about place to list your local business. Getting citations from many of the sites below (as well as ratings) can help boost your business listing in Google.

2. Yelp - The most popular social networking, directory, and review site. Aside from counting as a citation for your business in the eyes of major search engines, this site can deliver quite a bit of traffic on its own. However, business owners using Yelp will need to learn to deal with the occasional nasty review.

10. Foursquare - A popular way to check in to various locations using a smartphone. This can also provide a valuable citation for your local business.

3. Universal Business Listing - A local listing service – UBL.org (along with Localeze below) is one of the major players in the effort to only fill in your information once while getting listed on multiple yellow pages sites, directories and social networking/review sites. It saves time and effort but may be slower than going directly with the individual sites (see Localeze and InfoUSA below).

4. Yahoo Local - Yahoo's local directory is integrated with Yahoo Maps.

5. Local.com - Business listings, event listings, coupons, and reviews

6. CitySearch - One of the most authoritative local directories.

7. Bing Places for Business - Bing's local business listing service integrated with maps of cities and towns.

8. DMOZ (Open Directory Project) - A free and authoritative index (in the eyes of Google) that is managed by volunteers.

9. Superpages - One of the many Internet Yellow Pages directories (IYP). Includes business listings, people search, reviews and local deals.

10. Localeze - A multiple local listing service

11. DataAxle - A multiple local listings service.

12. Your local Chamber of Commerce - Joining your local chamber of commerce can often get you a business listing (and a citation for local SEO purposes)

13. InsiderPage - Local directory and rating site.

14. Merchant Circle - Local directory and rating site.

15. Best of the Web - -A popular directory with free and paid listing options – specifically for local, they have a Best of the Web Local directory.

16. yellowpages.com - Internet yellow pages (also YP.com).

17. Judys Book - Social search and online yellow pages

18. business.com - Business.com provides business information but also has a business directory.

19. Better Business Bureau - Your local Better Business Bureaus will usually charge for membership and provide a

link to your business.

The list could keep going for several pages. I think you get the idea. Find great citation sources and get links back to your site.

Directory of service companies (includes a "seal of approval").

By securing these high-quality citations you will boost your authority and highly improve your probability of ranking in the Google Map Listings. The next critical step is to get online reviews!

How to Get Online Reviews: Real Reviews from your Real Customers in your True Service Area

The next critical component for getting ranked on Google Maps, after you've claimed and optimized your listing, you've established your N.A.P. and you've developed your citations across the web, is obtaining reviews. You need to have real reviews from your real customers in your true service area.

Keep it Real

First, I want to point out that you shouldn't fill the system with fake or fraudulent reviews. You do not want to create bogus accounts and post reviews to Google Map, Yelp, City Search, etc. just for the sake of saying you've got reviews. That's not going to help you. You need real reviews from your actual customers in your true service area.

You might be thinking "Well, how is that important?" or "How would Google know the difference?" Google is paying very close attention to the reviewer's profile.

If somebody is an active Google user and they've got a Gmail account, and they've got a YouTube channel, typically that's all connected to a Google profile.

Say that person with the active profile has had their account for seven years and actually happens to be located in your service area. If he or she writes you a review, it would be considered credible and will count in your favor.

Now, if somebody creates a Google account with the sole intent of writing a review, it obviously is not credible, and Google is capable of catching on to that. That account has no history associated with it and it was originated right at your office IP address. That review is going to be flagged as a bogus submission.

It is important to have an authentic strategy where you are connecting with real people who will write your reviews. You don't want to try and play the system. Google is fully aware, and so is Yelp and a number of other popular online review sites.

Getting Reviews

With that said, how can you get reviews? What kind of process will you need to actually get reviews from your real customers in your real service area?

Here's the strategy that we advocate

First of all, have some review cards printed up (a sample is referenced later in this chapter). It's basically just a simple document with your company logo, and a short and sweet thank you note.

"Thanks so much for your business. We appreciate the opportunity to serve you. We'd love it if you would write us a review." Then give them a link to a page on your website where they can write you a review.

You will want to do some homework on the front end. Be sure you have a page on your website that is clearly meant for reviews: yourcompany.com/reviews. On that page you'll have links to the various places where people can write your reviews.

You'll want to have a link to your Google Maps listing, Yahoo local listing, Angie's List listing, City Search listing and any others that you may have. The reason you want to really have a variety of places where people can write those reviews is twofold.

Yes, you want to have a lot of reviews on Google Maps. But Google is also looking at the reviews that you have on other websites like Yelp and Angie's List. They're looking at the reviews that you have on Yellow Pages and other pages.

You need to diversify where you're getting reviews from your customers. It looks more authentic to have 12 on Google and 17 on YP.com, than it does if you just have 72 reviews on Google Maps.

You want to make it easy and you want to give people options.

Make It Easy

The other thing you want to bear in mind is that different people use different systems.

I am personally a big Google user. If you sent me an email or gave me a card that said, "Please write me a review" and provide me with various options, I'm going to say, "OK, Google." Click Google. Write my review

Some people, however, don't have Google accounts. They're not active Google users, but they may be heavily involved in Angie's List or big-time reviewers on Yelp.

They're going to have active accounts somewhere. It would be much easier for them to write the reviews where they already have an existing account. The easier and more convenient you make it for people, the better. It's going to bode well in your favor.

Like we mentioned, Google is looking at the reviewer profile. If you only give them one option, and that's Google, but they happen to be a Yelp user without a Google account, they will have to go out of their way to create an account to write the review.

This is not likely to happen. But, let's say they did decide to create an account. That review is not going to count for much because there's no active profile.

By providing options, the Yelp user that has a reputation for writing reviews and decides to write one for you is going to make a difference. That review is going to stick as opposed to being filtered. Make it easy for them to choose the one that's going to be easiest for them.

Now Let's Get Back to the Strategy

Phase one, print out review cards. Have your technicians hand them out after a service. "Hey, thanks for your business. I just want to leave this with you. If you'd be willing to write us a review and share your experience, we would really appreciate it."

It's great. You're showing appreciation. You're holding yourself accountable because you're asking for feedback. By doing that on a consistent basis, you are likely to catch some fish.

The next thing you'll want to do, just to get a nice little bump in the number of reviews that you have, is to develop an email list of your circle of influence.

Your circle of influence is going to be your most recent customers, the customers that have been using your services for quite some time, your family members, and your friends. People that you know, like, and trust, who would be willing to act on your behalf.

Put together that email list in an Excel sheet. It might be ten contacts, or it might be 700 contacts. Include the names and email addresses of these folks. Then, use a tool like Constant Contact or MailChimp or another email marketing tool to send an email blast with the following message:

Email Subject" Thanks for your business!

Name,

I wanted to shoot you a quick email to thank you for your business and let you know how much we appreciate the opportunity to serve you!

Our goal is to provide 100% customer satisfaction and exceed your expectations every step of the way. I certainly hope that we did just that!

If so, it would really help us out if you'd be willing to post a review for us online at one of your favorite online review sites. Below are a few sample direct links where you could write a public review about your experience with us:

- Google Review Link
- Yelp Review Link

Thank you again! We really appreciate your support!

Best Regards, Owner

Again, save them the time of having to find the websites on their own by providing some links to the various places to where they can write reviews.

By sending this email, you're going to create a little bump in your online review profiles. Again, reviews are important. Getting ten reviews on your Google Business Profile is essential.

It makes a huge difference in how you rank, and it gives you a different perception in the mind of your consumers. You want to get to past that ten review threshold almost immediately.

Doing that helps you get real reviews from real people that have real online profiles. Again, you want to have a systematic process in place where you are asking for reviews on a consistent basis from the customers that you are serving on a daily basis. The best way to do that is to request an email address from your customers, either at point of service or after service.

Establishing your Email Database

The best way to build your email database is by offering something of value in exchange for the email address. This can be anything really, but it must be valuable. People are not stupid, and they know if that if they give you the email address you are going to be emailing them.

We like to help our clients think of creative ways to offer value in exchange for the email. For ALFs, this might look like a good checklist. Here are some examples:

- The Top 10 Things You Must Look For in a Great Assisted Living Facility
- 5 Creative Ways to Pay for Senior Living
- 10 Day Trips for Senior Citizens That Don't Require Walking

Think of this as the transitional call to action. Ideally, we want people to book tours, and when they book tours, we'll get their email address. If you're not getting the email address when they book tours, you should start immediately.

Conclusion:

If you follow these steps to properly claim your Google Business Profile listing, develop your authority via citation development, and put a systematic process in place to get real reviews from your real customers in your true service area, you will be well on your way to dominating the Google Map 3 Pack, as well as ranking on page one of Google's organic results.

7 WEBSITE CONVERSION FUNDAMENTALS - HOW TO ENSURE THAT YOUR WEBSITE CONVERTS VISITORS INTO LEADS

This chapter is all about website conversion fundamentals. We talk about how you need to set up your website, the messaging on your website and the navigational flow of your website to ensure maximum conversion and profitability from your entire online marketing effort.

The way I look at it is, you can have the best Pay Per Click campaign, search engine optimization, and rank in the Google Map 3 Pack. But, if the content and the structure of your website isn't set up in a way that's compelling for users, then it doesn't give them a reason to choose you over the competition, and it doesn't give them the information that they need to easily say, "You're the Assisted Living facility that I am going to call for help." It's just not going to do as well as it could.

I want to talk about how we can take the traffic we're going to get from organic and Pay Per Click strategies, and make sure that the website is illustrating the correct message so we can maximize the profitability and revenue of our online marketing strategies.

Conversion Fundamentals

Be real. I talked about how people resonate with real people. They like to see the company, the people that they are going t be talking with on the phone and that are going to be takin care of them or their loved ones. So, as often as you can, avoi stock photography. Get a picture of the owner, the team, you facility, and the outside areas of the facility.

These things really draw people in and it gets them to fee that they would be working with real people because that is th kind of business that people want to deal with.

As for the content of your website, write messaging tha draws them in and makes them connect. They're looking for home where they or their loved ones are going to spend thei golden years, so when they land on your home page, the firs message they see should enforce the fact that they can trust you

You should write something along the lines of, "Are yo looking for a place that you can call home? Then you've com to the right place. We're operating on the same principles fo the last 30 years: trust, loving care, and excellence."

Connect with them. Give them reasons to choose you an have a call to action, "Give us a call at this number fo immediate service," or, "Click here to schedule a tour or take virtual tour of our facility." Remember, they've browsed aroun the Internet and have seen that there are several choices the can choose from in your area.

Give them some compelling information about who you ar and why they would want to choose you. Ask them to call no for a tour, and then draw them into a section where they can ge an offer or a special discount. This is going to incentivize then to choose you and make that call right away.

What to Write

When it comes to the copy on the website, you want to address their specific concerns.

For example, on the home page, write something generic, "Looking for an Assisted Living Facility You Can Trust?" You should also sympathize with them. "I know how important it is to find a home where you know you'll be taken care of. You need to make sure that you or your loved one is getting the right assistance."

Write that kind of messaging for each one of the pages on your website including a clear call to action after every block of text saying, "Call now to schedule your tour," or, "Click here to see our virtual tour of our facility."

Pull them deeper into your website with "About Us" links, special move in offers and blog content that might address their specific question.

Give them content that makes them think, "These guys know what they're doing," and draw them deeper and deeper into the website so they're more inclined to take the next step. Tell them why they should choose you over the competition. I talked about this in the "Message Market Media" chapter.

You should also, of course, have a web form on each of the pages of your website or, at a minimum, on the "Contact Us" page.

This is so that if they're not ready to pick up a phone, they can simply type in their name, email address, and phone number and let you contact them. Again, make sure that you've got your phone number on the top right-hand corner and that you've got a clear call to action telling them what to do next on every page of your website, under every block of text.

You'll want to display your authority on your homepage in one of the sections. You can do this with reviews and logos of associations that your facility may belong to.

Explain why they should choose you. Leverage personality. Be authentic. Integrate your photos into your website. It really, really helps with conversion.

Utilize your reviews, testimonials and videos. There's no reason you can't create a simple video for each of the pages on your website, explaining what the service is, and why your business can do it best.

Some people are visual, they can see the content on the website, read it and feel fine. Other people are more audible and would prefer to hear the message.

If you can spend the time to provide both text and video, it really helps with conversion. Give them external proof. Take them out to the review sites where they can preview testimonials on Caring.com, A Place for Mom, Google Business Profile.

Show them what other people are saying, and you're going to significantly improve your conversion.

Components of a Site That is Built to Convert

Internet marketing involves a lot of little things that are performed in sequence to get people to call your Assisted Living Facility when they are in need of your service. At the end of the month, it all comes down to the amount of calls you received and how much business was booked, right?

1. Company logo should always be in the top left hand side

of the page. Their logo here is the perfect size. Sometimes clients tell me they want their logo to be triple this size. The reality is that few searchers know you from your company name, so occupying too much space with just your logo is a waste of valuable webpage real estate.

2. Your phone number is VERY IMPORTANT for the credibility of your company. It should be as close to the top right hand corner as possible. Make sure it's large and easy to find. Try not to make people search for it. It's frustrating for searchers and you have just a few seconds for them to find it before they may move on to another website. People always look to the top of the page for that vital piece of info.

3. Professionally shot photos. For a small investment, you could and should have a professional photographer come in and take some photos. You will use them everywhere. DIY photography is ok, but a professional photo is so much better. You generally want to have smiley-happy people on your website, and we always prefer them to be real people from your facility.

4. A small blurb of text confirming the family-owned and operated company really brings it all together. People buy from people, not hidden companies. Personalize your website as much as possible. Your website is a marketing tool and its job is lead capture and to bring down as many buying barriers as possible.

5. Main navigation. Your website's main navigation should be easy to find and the links should be clearly descriptive. Give people the option of moving around your website. One of Google's algorithms is how many pages a person visits and what their visit length was. Guide them down a path without confusing them. In other words, give them all the information they need in as few clicks as possible, but

provide them the option of navigating around your site. Sometimes it is helpful to put certain links in the footer of the site. The footer is the bottom of each page. Pages like the privacy policy or terms and conditions might go there.

6.   Some people want a way to contact you without calling. A contact form above the fold (the top half of the page) is great for capturing clients' info. You can get a lot of form submissions on a monthly basis. It's also a great tool for building a contact list for email marketing down the road.

7.   Get to the point right away without going into too much detail. The first paragraph of your text should give you a brief introduction of who you are and what you do. You can go into further detail on your About Us page.

8.   Social media icons are a great tool because it allows potential visitors to see another side of your company. It's a great place to publish more videos and photos. Also, it's a great place to see how your company interacts with its community. From an SEO point of view, it helps build your company's social signal, something Google is paying more attention to. Social media is no longer just sexy "marketing speak", it is a must when it comes to online marketing.

9.   Your site has to be mobile friendly. Over 50% of users will be visiting your site from their iPhone or Android. You cannot afford to have a site that is not optimized for mobile users. Users will hit the back button faster than you can say "lost   customer".

***If you site isn't Mobile-Friendly, you need a new one.

Website Conversion Factor Analysis

I have summarized the positive and negative points of the website that can affect the User-Friendly Interface of the website and the website conversions.

Homepage Hero Section (Above the fold)

First, "Above the Fold" should be properly optimized. Above the fold areas are the sections of the webpage that are visible without the need for scrolling. You must pass the grunt test. The grunt test is whether or not a caveman could land your website and grunt what it is you do to help Seniors survive and thrive.

This space is critical in regard to the user engagement and as such the most appealing attributes should be showcased in this section. Some of the most important conversion factors that should be present in the above the fold section is the following:

- Attention grabbing headlines that are clear
- Bullet points
- Calls to Action that are direct and not passive
- Form   to   capture   leads

Second, you must include a proper section for "User Engagement" in the "above the fold" section of the website.

Ideally in the header section, there should be a downloadable PDF that provides value to the user, with an interesting title with a "Download Now" button and the user can download the same if they input their name and email address.

Other Sections on The Homepage

Problem Section

After the hero section (what's above the fold), I like to introduce the problem. You are reminding the user why they even came to your website. In the case of an Assisted Living

Facility, the headline might sound something like this: "Finding a Home for Mom or Dad is Really Hard"

After we introduce the problem we might use bullet points to agitate the problem and open story-loops in the user's mind. For example:

- Are you worried that Mom or Dad won't be cared for?
- Are you worried there won't be enough social activity?
- Are you still unsure about COVID and current protocols for ALFs?

We could keep going with different versions of the problem and how that problem might be making your potential customer feel.

Value Proposition

At this point your site visitor is likely seeing themselves in the story you're telling. Now you can use the next section to tell them how you solve the problem you introduced in the previous section. Your healing might sound something like this: Earning the Trust of Families For Over 20 Years

That headline speaks directly to the main problem of trust. Can the family trust you and your facility with their loved one. It also speaks to your authority of having been around for two decades.

Guide Section

In the guide section we want to speak with empathy and authority. You must let them know that you understand what they are feeling. Use the words, "We understand this search can be gut wrenching and scary. We've experienced this on a personal level and talk to families just like yours on a daily basis."

You can hear the empathy, right?

You follow the empathy with your authority as an Assisted Living Facility that can deliver the trust and care that people deserve. You might say something like: "This is why we've been helping families in the Dallas area for over 20 years house and care for their parents. We've been recognized as one of the top ALFs for the last 4 years and we belong to the Texas Assisted Living Association. On top of that we have 24 hour medical assistance in our facility."

You can hear the authority, right? If your facility is the best, this is the place to remind the user that they've found the right place. In this section you need to include a direct call to action button with "Book a Tour" on it.

Plan Section

Humans need a plan. Think of every action move you've ever seen. Somewhere in the story, one of the characters will say these words, "Okay, here's the plan." That is what you're doing with the plan section.

We want to be told what to do. Especially in a case where someone is looking for housing for their Mom or Dad. You do this with language like, "It's Easy to Get Started with Mercy House"

Following the headline, you might use a sub-head that says, "Simply follow the steps below and get one step closer to finding the home you need"

Now you want to give them an easy 3 step plan to get moved-in. We all know that it takes more than 3 three steps, but here we need to give them 30,000 foot level. It might look something like this:

1.   Discovery Call - On this call we'll discuss your specific

needs and go over how we might be able to help you and your family.

2.   Tour the Facility - There's nothing like seeing things for yourself. We're proud to show off our facility. We do it every week on Tuesday and Thursday.

3.   Welcome Home - Moving in is a cinch. We've got a checklist and process to make sure everything goes smoothly.

This plan works!! It's simple and step three is forward looking and foreshadows success!

Blog

A blog is useful as it gives the visitors useful information and also gives credibility to the business as the visitor perceives that the business is up to date with the happenings in the industry.

Also in regards to the recent algorithm changes, updating the home page content at regular intervals is critically important in regards to getting higher rankings in SERP's.

This is the reason the website should have a blog section in the home page similar to the following and the blogs should be updated regularly.

Testimonials

Testimonials are important since they earn credibility from your users. We like to embed Google reviews from your Google Business profile. This sends a strong signal to Google, as well as the people browsing your site.

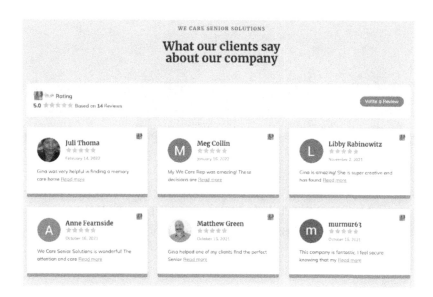

Testimonials are also another form of authority. Below is an image of site where we've embedded Google reviews right onto one of our customers homepage.

8 MOBILE OPTIMIZATION - HOW TO OPTIMIZE YOUR WEBSITE FOR MOBILE VISITORS

More and more of your customers are searching for service providers via mobile devices. Here are just a few eye-opening mobile stats you should be aware of:

- Up to 50% of web traffic happens on a mobile device (Source: Statista, 2021)
- 80% of users used a mobile device to search the internet in 2019 (Google)
- By 2026, the number of smartphone users is projected to reach 7.51 billion. (Source Statista)
- World Advertising Research Center predicts that by 2025, three-quarters (¾) of users will access the Internet using a mobile device.
- More than 4 out of 10 of all emails are opened on mobile devices. (Source: Statista, 2021)
- 82% of smartphone shoppers conduct "near me" searches. (Source: Uberall, 2018)
- It is predicted that mobile ad spending will reach almost 413 billion dollars by 2024. (Source: Statista)
- 61% of users will have a more positive opinion about your business if you have a good responsive website. (Source: Smart Insights, 2019)
- 57% of users say they wouldn't recommend a company

if their mobile website design is bad. (Google)
- By 2025, 44.2% of all eCommerce sales will be mobile sales. (Source: Business Insider)
- According to BrizFeel, 55.4% of users use their mobile devices for shopping. (Source: Oberlo)
- 50% of B2B search queries in 2017 were made on smartphones and that number is expected to continue growing (Google)
- 96% of Facebook users access the app via a mobile device (Google, 2020)

Mobile smartphones can access websites, as well as perform a multitude of other tasks, which is why they have become more of a necessity than a luxury these days.

For you, as a business owner, this provides a unique opportunity to connect with local customers via their mobile devices.

Before you start to develop a mobile arsenal to drive more inbound calls, you must first figure out who your mobile competitors are. It is important to know who you are up against in mobile marketing so you can plan your strategies accordingly.

To effectively do this, you need to identify your closest competitors and learn what mobile techniques they are using to generate their sales.

Mobile-Optimized Websites

First, find out which of your competitors have a mobile-optimized website. One quick and easy way to find out is to pull up their website on your mobile phone.

Did it load quickly? Was it easy to find their contact information and other details that consumers tend to look for while on-the-go? Was it optimized to fit your phone screen? If so, they have invested in their business by making sure their mobile customers and prospects are taken care of.

Now, pull up your website on your mobile phone. If it's nightmare, it's not your phone that is the problem, it's your website. This means you have been losing potential business.

Text Message Marketing

Next, figure out which of your competitors are using text message marketing. If your competitors are doing it, they are probably telling the world to "text 123 to example." If you see promotions such as this, they are using text messaging to build list of repeat customers.

This is one of the most cost-effective and results-oriented forms of marketing today. Text message marketing allows your competition to draw in local consumers with a great offer. Then they send out occasional messages or coupon offers to keep them coming back to use their services.

Let's say one of your customers had plans to contact your business today after work, but they recently joined your closest competitor's mobile list and had received a text coupon offer from them before they had the chance…

Who do you think the customer will call?

There are many other forms of mobile marketing your competitors could be using to capture the attention of local consumers such as mobile SEO, QR codes, and mobile apps.

If they are using these methods, it may be in your best interest to start researching how your business can do it even better.

Analyze Your Current Mobile Marketing Status

What is your status when it comes to staying connected with local consumers using Mobile Marketing strategies?

Researching your competition is a necessary task if your goal is to become the local authority in your niche. But it is equally important for you to analyze where your business currently stands in order to move forward.

Are you currently running a mobile marketing campaign, but not seeing the results you want? Or, do you want to start a mobile marketing campaign but keep putting it off because you don't know where to begin?

Every business in your local area is in a crucial fight for more customers and profits. Therefore, to enjoy a spike in sales, your company can no longer ignore the profitability of ramping up your mobile efforts.

Analyze Your Mobile Status

Many business owners pump a lot of muscle in competing with similar businesses while neglecting to take a close look at what they're doing.

Analyzing your mobile status will help you figure out which weaknesses are holding you back and which strong points can help you win the war.

You need to understand where your past efforts have taken you, as well as what your future has in store for you based on where you stand today.

For starters, you must take note of what you are and aren't doing to generate more sales using mobile marketing.

Ask yourself the following:
- Is your mobile website user-friendly? Does it load within seconds or take forever to render properly? Does your mobile website have all the relevant information on it that consumers look   for   while   on   the   go?

- Does your mobile website come up high in the rankings on mobile search engines, or is it nowhere to be found when local consumers perform a search for your "service + your city"   on   their   mobile   devices?

- Have you started to build a text marketing list? If so, what   are   you   currently   doing   with   that   list?

- Is your opt-in/call-to-action on all of your printed and web   marketing   materials?

Are you using QR codes as an additional method of increasing awareness about your business? Do you have your QR codes on all your other marketing materials? Are you using them   to   direct   traffic   to   your   mobile   website?

As you can see, there are a lot of things to consider when it comes to making sure your business is on the right track toward beating your local competition with mobile marketing.

Spy   on   Your   Mobile   Marketing   Competitors

Do you want to know how your closest competitors are driving more business by using mobile marketing? Just take a look at their campaign yourself.

Mobile marketing has recently opened new doors for businesses that want to market their products and services by using mobile phones as personal "mini billboards". This has been enhanced by the fact that more and more people own mobile devices, and use them to find local products, services, and businesses regularly.

To beat your competitors in the world of mobile marketing, you need to know what they are doing to be ahead of the curve. Digital technology is growing at astonishing rates and is not expected to slow down anytime soon.

This alone is causing many companies to be left behind when it comes to new-age technology.

Spying on your competitors' mobile marketing initiatives may seem like a daunting task, but it's not. All you need to do is identify which are taking most of your customers and let the research begin.

You should begin by visiting their mobile websites on your phone. Go through the websites and take note of the look and feel, the features, and the traffic flow. Although your goal is NOT to copy exactly what they're doing, you could get a few pointers for your own mobile website.

Next, find out how their text message marketing campaigns operate simply by joining their mobile list. They probably have a text call-to-action placed everywhere, so opt-in and pay close attention to what happens throughout the entire process. This is the perfect way to get a first-hand look at their services, products, and promotions.

Are your competitors using QR codes to generate interest in their business? If so, whip out your mobile phone and scan their codes to see what lies behind them. Where do the QR codes take you? What type of incentives are they offering to get people to scan them?

Another thing you can investigate is your competitors' mobile applications. Download their apps and see what they're offering and how user-friendly they are.

The information you gain from your research should be used solely to set up your mobile marketing campaign that not only beats your competitors but also attracts new customers and keeps them loyal to your business.

Spying on your competitors is not illegal, but there are limits you should follow to remain fair. Under no circumstances should you use unethical measures to jeopardize your competition in your quest for mobile marketing.

Make Customers Call Your Business with Mobile Marketing

The secret to beating your competitors in the business is making your company more interesting to your target audience. There are several ways to do this using mobile marketing if you plan ahead, focus on the right things, and maintain your campaigns over time.

As much as you would like to boot your local competitors out of the picture, the fact is a lot of them will probably be using some of the same mobile marketing methods as you are.

So, your main focus should be geared toward making your customers choose your business over theirs. This is fairly easy to do if your efforts are consistent and persistent.

It is up to you which tools you use to work positively toward attracting new customers and keeping the ones you already have.

Here are a few tips which can work in your favor and help

local consumers choose you:

- You need to have a good website that is mobile-friendly and easily accessible by mobile phone users in your area. People are using their mobile phones to access the web to search for local products and services while on the go. Make sure your site loads quickly, gives them the exact information they need, and is easy to navigate.

- If you choose to start a text message marketing campaign, make sure your text messages offer great value, relay a clear message, and are short and informative. Also, be sure to send messages out consistently, yet conservatively. Create a careful balance that makes sense for your business and your target audience. Need a boost in getting new mobile subscribers? Give your customers and prospects a great incentive in exchange for opting-in and watch your list grow exponentially.

- Consumers love businesses that stay "on top" of the digital age. They expect you to have a website, be actively involved in their favorite social media outlets, and be easily accessible from their mobile devices. Have a mobile app developed to aid in keeping your local consumers connected with your business. Implement the use of QR codes as a way to keep your local consumers engaged and provide them with "instant gratification."

- Mobile SEO should be used effectively to attract qualified traffic to your website. Mobile users search for local products and services constantly on their mobile devices when on the go. If your business does not rank in the results, there is a major potential profit leak left for your competitors to scoop up.

Finding Your Business Basics

If somebody goes online, searches for your services, and get to your website, they probably want to just get the basi information. They probably are not interested in learning a to of information about you. They simply want to find who yo are, where you're located, what your services are, and then pres a button to book a service.

I have an example below of a mobile version of a site wher they can just get the basic information, hit that "Book a Appointment" button, and then schedule an appointment. Yo should absolutely set up a mobile version of your site, give th basic information, and don't overcomplicate it.

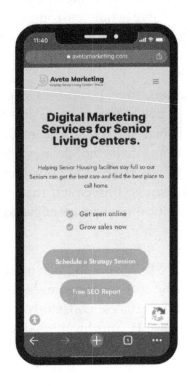

9 SOCIAL MEDIA MARKETING - HOW TO LEVERAGE SOCIAL MEDIA FOR MAXIMUM EFFECT FOR YOUR ALF

It's settled. Social Media is here to stay and it works to promote business (Facebook, Twitter, YouTube, LinkedIn), but how can it be leveraged by an Assisted Living Facility? How can you use social media to grow your business?

In this chapter, we are going to cover social media marketing for your business. I hope that by now, you've learned a lot about how to position your company online, how to rank well on the organic listings on the Google Map 3 Pack.

Now, we're going to talk about social media marketing, and how you can utilize social media tools like Facebook, Twitter, and LinkedIn to grow your business.

As I talk to business owners throughout the country about Internet marketing and social media, I tend to get a puzzled look. The question is, "How in the world does all of this social media stuff apply to my business? How can I possibly use Facebook in a way that would help me increase my revenues, boost my service calls, and get more repeat business?"

I'd like to try and bridge the gap on where the "lowest-hanging fruit" for social media is in your business by asking, "What's your number one source of business today?"

Just stop and think, where does most of your revenue come from? You'll quickly come to the conclusion that your number one source of revenue is repeated and referral business. The lifeblood of any service business is your existing customers returning for services over time, and your existing customers referring you to their friends and family. If social media is harnessed correctly, it gives you the ability to take that repeat and referral business, inject it with steroids, and take it to a whole new level.

Let me explain why I feel that it's a great place for you to really connect with your customers and get more repeat and referral business. Just a couple of Facebook stats gleaned from Google:

- Facebook currently has 2.91 billion users
- The average user has 338 friends
- Users check in an average of 14 times per day

If you can get your real customers, current and past (your sphere of influence) to connect with you on social media, such as Facebook and/or Twitter, your business is exposed to their 388 friends as soon as they "like" and follow your page.

It's almost as if they'd sent an email, or they'd sent a text message out to all their friends saying, "I recently received a service from this service provider in our area. The next time you need their services, why don't you think about them?" It's extremely powerful to gain exposure to their sphere of influence.

Another major advantage is that they've given you permission to remain top-of-mind with them. The average user, like I said, checks in 14 times per day. They login to check out the updates on their Facebook wall and to see the updates of all the companies and people they have liked or are friends with. If you're posting updates to your social media profiles, the people who have liked your page are going to see that new content whenever they login.

They are going to see an update and your logo. They're going to see some special offer or promotion, and it's going to pique their interest. When the time comes thatthey need your services, who do you think they're going to call?

Top of Mind Awareness

There is a higher probability folks who have liked your page are going to use you again, and refer you to their friends, because they remember you and had a good experience with your service offering. They know who you are.

You've remained top-of-mind. If you look at major companies like Coca Cola, Pepsi, and Lay's, they spend billions of dollars a year on advertising and promotions, through TV, radio, and print.

What's the whole thought process behind that? They're developing their brand, so they can maintain what we call "TOMA," top-of-mind awareness. Leveraging social media inside your existing sphere of influence is a great way to tap into that top-of-mind awareness.

Where should you start? Where can you start using social media, with all of the different platforms out there? With so many different social media tools, what should you be using?

In chapter two, we talked about having a blog and putting out consistent updates. Well, blogging ties very nicely to your social media strategy. These are the social media profiles you definitely want to have set up and ready to roll in your business.

Finding Your Followers

Let's talk strategy before we get into the granular details. Talk about high level. How do you leverage social media and how do you gain that initial following?

Well, first, you want to utilize email to get initial engagement. Having an active social media profile with daily updates is not worth a hill of beans if you don't have likes or views.

Now, at the same time, if you have thousands of irrelevant people that have pressed like on your website or on your Facebook profile, it's not going to work to your advantage if they're not people in your service area. They're not the target market that we discussed in the marketing fundamentals.

You want to make sure that you have a strategy to get your real customers and your true service area engaged with you in social media. You should leverage email to engage your customers to get to your social media profiles. This takes a multiple step process.

The first thing you want to do is build that list or go into your customer relationship management system, if you have one, and export the name and email addresses of your customers. Include current customers, past customers, sphere of influence of your friends, your business partners, the people that you do business with, and put them into an email.

Queue up a nice little message which says, "Hey, we appreciate your business. We appreciate your relationship over the years. We're getting active in social media and would love to have you engage with us. Please go to Facebook.com and pres the Like button." Make sure to give them a direct link to you Facebook page.

There are a couple of things you can do. You can offer ther an incentive, something of value like a coupon or a discoun Or, if you feel like you've got an active customer base th, knows who you are and likes you, just ask them to do it as favor.

You'll be able to start building that following. Now, yo don't want to stop there. You don't want to just send one ema out that says, "We're on social media." You now want to build as part of your business.

Just Ask!

In the Google Business Profile Optimization chapter, talked about having an email go out after service, thanking th customer for their business and asking them to go ahead an write a review for you on one of the various online director sites.

Well, there's no reason you couldn't send a subsequent ema to that contact, maybe a day or two later, which says, "By th way, we're actively involved in social media and would love it . you would engage with us." Then give them a direct link to you social media profiles where they can press like, subscribe, an follow to start engaging with you on social media.

The key is that it needs to be an automated process wher you're typing your customer's name and their email addres These emails go out to everybody that you serve without an hiccups, and without any potential for dropping the ball. If yo don't do it consistently, you won't get a true following - and yo won't get your real customers engaging with you on these soci, media platforms.

That's step one. Leverage email to build that initial engagement and following of your real customers. Remember, we want authentic customers, not just throwaway links and subscribers.

Once you've got that part squared away, you have got to think about what you are going to post. What information are you going to put up and how frequently? You should post to your social media profiles once a day. If that seems like too much for your business, post once a week at a very minimum.

What to Post (and Why)

These should be informative posts. It should not be a sales pitch. It should not be, "Here's 10-percent off your next service."

You can do that every now and then but more than 80% of the time it should just be social content: "Here's a picture of a kitchen that we remodeled", "This is what's going on in our market", "Here's a picture of us at the latest home show.", etc.

Keep it informational, keep it relevant, keep it social, and then you must engage. Social media isn't a one-way dialogue. You shouldn't be going to your social media profiles and pushing out updates that don't have any engagement. You shouldn't just be posting. You should be trying to get people to reply to your post: "Hey, that was funny", or "That's a beautiful picture", or "Thanks for that great tip," all of which you can reply back to.

Then, listen to what your fans are saying. Once you've got a flow – you've got 50, 70, 100 or a couple of thousand people that have liked you – you are going to be able to hear what they are saying as well. They might post something that's totally irrelevant to you, like "Hey, tomorrow's Billy's birthday." There is no reason that your organization couldn't reach out and say, "Hey, wish Billy a happy birthday for us!", from your company. They will think, "Wow, this is a company that cares. This is a company that's real and authentic."

Engaging in social media is probably a lost art. Most people that use social media just post one-way messages, which is not the idea. It's a social platform, so there should be conversation. There should be dialogue.

Fill in the Business Bio

The next thing you want to do is to develop your brand and make sure that you enhance the bio section on each one of these profiles. Within Facebook, Twitter and LinkedIn, you will have the option to fill in an 'About Us' or bio section. Write some interesting information about your business there.

Take the information from the 'About Us' page on your website where you talk about where you were founded, why you started the business, the service that you offer, etc., and pop that into the bio section on your social media profiles.

You also have the ability to put an icon on each one of these social profiles, and you want to make sure that you're using an image that represents your business. It can either be a head shot of the owner or it can be a logo. We often provide banners and badges that "on-brand" for our clients. You want the brand to feel right no matter where your clients or potential clients would see you on the internet.

It's all about branding, so make sure that you're leveraging the header graphic and the image icon. If there is an option for you to customize the background, do it! You want to make sure that your elements marry up with the overall branding of your business.

Make sure everything on your social media profiles is consistent with your website. On your website, you've got a color scheme, a logo, and maybe you have printed brochures. Be sure to keep a consistent flow, look, feel, and color scheme on all your social media profiles, website, and offline materials.

Posting Plans and Pointers

Don't forget to have a plan for social media. How often are you going to post? What types of posts are you going to put out there? Who is going to be responsible for posting them? How are you going to engage your customers? Which social media profiles is your business going to be involved with?

Remember in chapter two we talked about the fundamentals of your marketing plan (market, message and media). Be sure that you have a clear understanding of who your customer is and who your ideal customer is. Then make sure that you are crafting a message that will resonate with that particular customer. It's important to consider all of these things as part of your social media strategy.

Don't just dive in. A common mistake would be to just setup the profile and start posting with no thought process or plan behind it. Think about it. What pages are you going to be on? What message are you going to put out? What color scheme are you going to use? Set all of that up and then get very specific about your target. Is your client the commercial type? Is your client a residential type?

One solid method is to schedule your post types on specific days, such as:

Monday, Wednesday and Friday are the days that you are going to put up tips.

Tuesday and Thursday, you'll post images and videos from your community. Remember to always get permission from your guests and their families before you post any images or videos of residents.

Saturday and Sunday, you post coupons.

I am not saying this is the editorial calendar you must follow. This is only an example. However, the point is to make it easy for yourself so that you know what is going up and when. Your posting process can be streamlined, and it can also be automated.

Leveraging Posts

When we talked about the blog in the SEO chapter, we went over leveraging content. Because content is king, you have to be creating updated information on a consistent basis.

This content can go up in various places. As you post a new piece of content, it can go to your Facebook and Twitter pages automatically. It can go straight out to Pinterest if it has a photo included, and you can take your blog content and syndicate it to recreate great social media content.

Remember, content isn't necessarily just written text. You are an expert in your craft. You know things that the average consumer doesn't, such as what to do in the event of an emergency, why somebody would want to consider a specific service offering versus another, or why somebody would want to consider a new service offering you have recently started.

You can either sit down and write about it, you can take an audio recorder and record yourself talking about it, or if you're comfortable on video, you can break out the camera phone and shoot a video talking about an issue your ideal consumer may be facing.

How 1 Equals 5

Once you make a video, you can get a lot more bang for your buck. That one piece of content can serve multiple functions. The first function can be posting videos up on social media or on websites where you can upload interesting clips and videos like YouTube or Vimeo.

You can also have the video transcribed using a service like Rev or Descript. There are various transcription services available.

That video of you talking about the benefits of your service offering can now be transcribed into text, which may then be used as a blog post and be syndicated into your social media profiles. Another step beyond that is using that same audio and turning it into an audio podcast you can have hosted on your website.

There are a lot of things you could do to take your content and work with the modality that you're most comfortable with. Some people like to write. Some people like to talk. Some people like to be on video. Figure out what you are most comfortable with and run with that. This is how you create social media content for your online marketing plan.

Remember, educational content that's published in multiple places gives you industry expert status. By publishing and getting picked up in industry listings, the local newspaper or reputable blog, you are considered an expert. This is going t drive your credibility, which in turn, will result in more referrals

Do's and Don'ts of Posting:

1. Use the 80/20 rule for marketing messages. Put out 80% information and 20% marketing

2. Keep it business related. Your political and religious belief are never a good mix with busines

3. Photos of your kids playing tee ball are good, but don't let it dominate your page

4. Keep your vacation photos on your personal social sites

5. Keep your business opinions, beliefs, and interests t yourself.

Sometimes knowing what not to post is more important tha knowing what to post, because the natural tendency is to go t these social media profiles, and just post promotional material.

When and How to Engage

We talked about asking your customers to 'like you' o Facebook and asking your customers to write testimonials. W also talked about interaction and responding to your customer actions. "Hey, thanks so much for the follow. We appreciate it. Or, if they write you a testimonial, make sure you blow that up.

Not only should you say thank you, but you should als share it. "Hey, Jean, thanks so much for the positive testimonia We appreciate your feedback. We appreciate your business, an this is what keeps us going. This is what we're in this busines for."

Then, you could take the testimonial and put it on your website or embed it on your website through the various widgets and short codes that Facebook provides.

For example, you create a post saying, "Seniors should live at a place where they can maintain their normal lifestyles and follow their interests. Let us know how we can help." Then, one of your followers says, "Wonderful caring staff. So lovingly devoted to those they serve." Then you respond: "Thank you for your comment! Our office phone number is 254-555-5555. We look forward to answering any questions you may have!"

This is your engagement. You want people to make comments, and then you want to be able to talk back.

This is just a way to put out relevant content, and if you're paying attention to your feed, you can turn it into some great conversation. Again, you want to be active on social media.

It's a great way to get repeat or referral business. You need to be on Facebook, LinkedIn, Twitter and YouTube. You want to utilize email marketing to gain that initial following, and then post updates that are informative and not sales-oriented on a consistent basis and engage.

If you do this regularly and correctly, you're going to grow a nice following of real customers in your true service area. You're going to remain top-of-mind and it's going to help you grow your business in terms of the lifeblood of your organization, which is repeat and referral business.

How to Avoid Mistakes on Facebook

With more than 500 million users, Facebook has become a must-use marketing platform for businesses of all sizes. While

Facebook's staggering membership stats alone are enough to entice small business owners, few actually know how to do so effectively.

Here are 10 of the most common Facebook marketing mistakes business owners make and how you can avoid them.

Not having a clear marketing purpose: Whether you've created a page for Facebook or are still working on it, now is a good time to evaluate what you want to get out of it. So set clear goals at the very beginning.

For example, suppose you are hoping to attract 500 new fans who could become potential customers in a six-month time period. Be sure to assign someone within your company to maintain the page. It's important to regularly post fresh content in the page. If you've already created your page, but it hasn't been updated in a while, be sure to update.

Not knowing the difference between a personal profile and a business page: There are so many major differences between personal and business pages on Facebook. You should know what they are so that you stay safely within Facebook's Terms of Service.

A personal profile is the type of account an individual shares with friends and family. But a Facebook business page is used by brands and companies for promotion purposes.

Another important distinction: If you have a Facebook page for your business, you have fans. If you have a personal profile, you've got friends. So, don't ask your potential customers to become your "friend" on Facebook. They need to become a fan.

Not understanding how your customers use Facebook: Many

small business owners don't know how their customers interact with Facebook. When you log into your Facebook account, for instance, the first thing you see is your news feed. You don't see the pages that you've liked.

It's important to understand that marketing your business page is not the same as posting a status update to your friends through your personal Facebook account. If you want to get your fans to view your content, you need to post directly to the Facebook page for your business. Your posts will show up in your news feed and will also show up in theirs.

Not getting the right URL for your Facebook page: You also need to know how to obtain the proper URL for your business page on Facebook. There are so many business owners who don't understand that if you have 25 fans of your business page, you are eligible to obtain a URL for your page that has your company's name in it.

For example, it could be www.facebook.com/yourcompanyname instead of the former random number URL assigned. You can go directly to www.facebook.com/username and log in to choose your URL.

Not responding to wall posts: It is a smart idea to remember that Facebook is all about interaction. It's very important you quickly respond to potential customers if they post questions on your wall.

The faster you can answer their question, the higher the likelihood of converting that potential customer into a paying one. You can adjust your Facebook page settings to notify you via e-mail whenever a new post is made on your wall.

Creating fake Facebook user accounts to boost fan count: It is a long-term process to get potential customers and existing ones to become fans of your business Facebook page. Although you may want to see your fan count increase rapidly, don't give in to the temptation to create fake Facebook accounts and then become a fan of your business page using that particular account. Facebook can often detect fake accounts, which are a violation of their Terms of Service. If you're caught, you will lose your page and the marketing power that comes with it.

Not updating the page regularly: You should not create a page for your business and let it become inactive. You should update it with fresh content at least two times a week. This will help keep your fans engaged and interested in your brand.

Posting poor quality content: Nothing irritates a potential customer like poor content. Consumers are always looking for useful information, not hype. Before you post anything, you should ask yourself how your content benefits your fans. If you can't answer that question, revise before you post it.

Not using Facebook's free tools: One of the great things about Facebook is that it offers several free tools to help businesses gauge how well they are using their page to attract and engage customers. There are many free tools in Facebook that provide business owners with detailed metrics about the effectiveness of their page content, analysis of user growth and demographics, and other concerns. You can find out more about it by logging on to https://developers.facebook.com/docs/platforminsights/page.

Not properly promoting your page: Many business owners aren't aware of the ways in which they can promote their Facebook page and attract potential customers. Facebook offers an advertising option that allows you to purchase relatively inexpensive ads.

You can also purchase a paid sponsorship of your post. For example, if you've written a post about the best strategies for designing a good website, you can promote that post on Facebook through its advertising and sponsorship platform. You can also create a link to your Facebook page on your company website.

10 LEVERAGE EMAIL MARKETING TO CONNECT WITH YOUR CUSTOMERS ON A DEEPER LEVEL, GET MORE REVIEWS, MORE SOCIAL FOLLOWERS AND ULTIMATELY MORE BUSINESS

Ever since there's been email, there's been email marketing. Email marketing is one of the oldest forms of advertising your business on the Internet.

Although it gets a bad rap because of all the spam going around, it's still one of the most effective forms of marketing.

I am a big believer in email marketing. It's a powerful way to get instant traffic to your website and getting the telephone to ring, but there is a right way and a wrong way to use it.

Did you know the easiest customer to sell to is the customer you already have?

Every self-proclaimed marketing expert will tell you that's nothing new. With that said, many business owners hardly ever market or keep in touch with their existing client base. Companies will spend thousands of dollars trying to get new customers but never think to market to the clients who already buy from them.

Why is that? I have a lot of ideas about this. I suspect business owners think that once a customer buys from them, they will just keep coming back on their own. Or maybe they simply don't want to bother their customers. The truth is customers want to hear from you and they want to be touched by your business. If you don't, your competition will.

How Do We Start an Email Marketing Campaign?

The first thing you need is an email marketing service. You shouldn't do this yourself for several reasons:

1. Your Internet Service Provider (ISP) will blacklist you for sending bulk mail.
10. You would have no stats for tracking your open emails
11. It would look unprofessional coming from your Microsoft Outlook box

With that said, let's take a look at some of the popular email marketing services, all of which are paid services and are priced based on the amount of emails you send. Many of these services have a free plan that actually delivers a lot of value, and you'd only start paying once you started sending 1000s of emails.

ActiveCampaign
I have used ActiveCampaign for many automated nurture series emails. They have a pretty good user interface that is fairly intuitive and great customer support. They have a free plan that includes an automated nurture series.

MailChimp
Mailchimp is another service I have personally used and recommend. It's relatively easy to use and offers similar features to Constant Contact. The interface is clean and easy to use, and

last I checked they have a free plan as well.

Mailerlite

I've used Mailerlite personally and have helped several clients use it as well. It's good and has a free plan. It is fairly easy to use and navigate and customer support is decent.

How to Get Email Addresses

I am asked on a regular basis about how to get email addresses. It's not as easy as sending a letter in the USPS mail to anyone you want to. The reality of it is that just because they are your customer and you have their email address doesn't mean you can send them anything if you don't have their permission.

This certainly is a fine line, because you somehow already have their email address, and they have used your services before, so is it really considered spam? Technically, yes. You didn't ask them if you could send them specials or a newsletter in email form.

The first thing you really want to do is get your clients' permission to add them to your email list. There are a variety of ways to do this, including placing a form on your website, putting a sign-up sheet on your counter or even a putting a space on your job ticket that they sign when you complete your service.

Explain that you send out tips about your industry or specials on a monthly basis and would love to have them on your mailing list. You might even offer a discount coupon off your services if they sign up.

Getting that email address is valuable, so if it cost you 5%, go for it. Remember, you want the opportunity to have your company's name in front of your customers every single month.

You want to remain top-of-mind if one of their friends is looking for services like yours or if they run into an emergency.

I had a pest control service provider come to my home several years ago. He did a good job and was very professional.

Four or five years later, I needed the services of the company again. I lost his business card and could not remember the name of the company. I had to find another pest removal service. He lost the business because he never stayed in contact with me. It was a big job that he lost, $1,500.00 to be exact.

Start building your list today.

What to Send and How Often

First, what do I send? You must use the 80/20 rule, 80 percent good information and 20 percent sales. If all you send is emails about what services you offer, no one will ever read it. It's a great way to kill your list.

Draft up some information about your industry, give good homeowner tips, throw in some DIY tips, and make sure it's information that will help your users. For the 20% sales, add a coupon or a special you are having, or offer something for your customers' friends and family.

How often you send your emails is very important. I always go with once per month, around the same time every month.
It is important to commit to a date. More than once a month is too much and annoys people.

I get an email from a company I purchased from in the past and get 3-4 emails a week from them, 100% sales, sometimes several times a day. I HATE IT and it drives me nuts. I removed myself from that list very quickly as I'm sure others have as well.

Get Legal

Make sure you have allowed customers the option to Opt Out of receiving email messages at the bottom of every message. Many of the email sending platforms will force you to do this because they want to keep their sending reputation good as well.

Make sure that it's easy because nothing is more annoying than receiving emails that you don't want. If someone does not want to receive your messages, then remove them from your list.

They may be getting emails from too many sources and just want to clean out their email box. It does not mean they will never buy from you again. But I will tell you this, if they want out and you keep sending email to them, it's a sure-fire way to bother them and they will likely never buy from you again.

Again, you want to leverage email marketing as part of your overall Internet marketing strategy. The best way to use it is to be sure you're collecting the email address from all your customers and prospects.

From there, use email marketing to get online reviews, engagement on your social media accounts and remain top-of-mind as a strategy to get more repeat and referral business.

What is the Best Time to Send an Email Campaign?

These general email send time tips are widely accepted by the email marketing community. They are great when you're starting off, but be sure to read on and see why they won't always work.

- Day-time vs. Night-time. While this one may be obvious, it's usually better to send out your email campaigns during the daytime. You know, when people are awake. Not asleep.

- Mad Mondays. The general consensus is that you should avoid sending out email blasts on Mondays. Why? People are already bummed out about the end of the weekend. They march into the office and are flooded with emails they've collected over the past few days. What's the first thing they do?   Delete   those   emails   of   course!

- Weekends. Historically, weekends are the days when folks are out running errands and going on adventures. Weekends tend to have low open rates, so most marketers avoid   them   like   the   plague.

- Fan   Favorites: Tuesday,   Wednesday,   and Thursday. Tuesday, Wednesday, and Thursday have traditionally been favorite days to send email campaigns, as email marketers seek to avoid the Monday angst and Friday's itchy feet. MailChimp confirms that Tuesday and Thursday are the two most popular days to send email newsletters.

11 MAXIMIZE PPC (PAY PER CLICK) FOR YOUR ASSISTED LIVING FACILITY

In this chapter, we're going to talk about Pay Per Click Marketing to help you understand how it works, why it should be integrated into your overall strategy, and how you can run a really effective program that can drive a nice, profitable business for your Assisted Living Facility.

Why PPC Should be a Part of Your Overall Online Marketing Strategy

- Start showing up quickly
- Show up as often as possible where your customers are looking
- Show up for non-geo modified terms that are related to your service offering

First, PPC gets things happening quickly, unlike an SEO program, setting up your website, building links and having the right on-page optimization. That process takes a little bit of time to materialize. What you do today and tomorrow, will start to pay dividends in three to four months.

With PPC advertising, you set up your campaign and will start to see your ads serve in just a few days. It can drive good traffic especially during the times when you need to make sure you're visible. We looked at the differences between the paid listings, the organic listings and the map listings.

You want to show up as often as possible when someone's looking for your services. Having a pay per click ad that shows up somewhere in the top, on the map, and in the organic section is important.

Now you've got the opportunity to show up in multiple places and significantly improve the chances of getting your ad clicked on, as opposed to your competition. A pay per click campaign gives you that additional placeholder on the search engines on page one.

It also gives you the opportunity to show up for words that you're not going to show up for in your organic SEO efforts. This is what I like to call non geo-modified keywords.

SEO and our whole organic strategy give us the ability to show up in search engines when someone types in your city service, for e.g. your city assisted living facility, your city memory care, your city senior housing, etc. All of those include some kind of geo modifier (your city). They're going to put their city or their sub-city in that search for you to rank.

With a PPC campaign, you can show up for the non-geo-modified terms (Example: family dentist, accounting, interior painting, exterior painting, caulking, priming, etc.), and put in the settings that you only want to show up for people within a 25-mile radius of your office.

If you're in Dallas and somebody searches within that area for "assisted living facility" or "memory care," you can set it so that it only shows your ad for the people that are searching within that area. And Google can manage that through IP addresses by isolating where the search took place.

Google can also isolate who ran that search, where they ran that search from, and then place the ads based on the advertisers that are set up for that area.

You only pay on a per click basis, but you're able to show up for those keywords in those major markets. Another reason that you want to consider running a pay per click campaign is because you can run mobile PPC campaigns.

With mobile PPC campaigns, when somebody is searching for your services from a mobile device, it's typically because they need immediate service. They're not as apt to browse multiple pages or listings. Now, if somebody runs a search on their mobile device, and you have a pay per click campaign set up, that search will be PPC enabled.

They can simply hit your ad and automatically be calling your company, rather than browsing to your website and researching.

On a pay per click campaign through mobile, you're actually paying per call as opposed to paying per lead. It's very powerful, and these are the reasons you want to have pay per click as part of your overall Internet marketing plan.

The Pay Per Click Networks

So, what are the pay per click networks? There are two major networks that manage pay per click advertising across almost all the major search engines. There's Google Ads, which is Google's pay per click program, and then there is Microsoft Advertising (Bing).

These both have their own network behind them, so when you pay for an ad or pay per click campaign on Google's search network, you're gaining access to AOL, AT&T, USA Today, and Ask.com.

When you get on the Microsoft Advertising search network, you're getting access to Yahoo!, Facebook, etc. There are a variety of reasons to consider a Microsoft Advertising pay per click strategy.

You can review the chart above to see where most people search and what's going to give you the most attention. It clearly shows that Google is the dominant player with no serious competition.

More than 80 percent of all searches happen on Google.com. So, if you had to choose, you would obviously you want to use Google. However, you do get an additional 20 percent by tapping into Microsoft (Bing) and Yahoo!.

There are different networks but those two make up the majority of the search market. Running a pay per click campaign on both Google Ads and Microsoft (Bing) search will allow you to show up in the majority of the search engines that somebody might be using.

Understanding the Google AdWords Auction Process

Let's review how Google Ads works.

In the simplest sense, you're paying on a per click basis and you can choose your keywords (Example: dentist, your city dentist, your city emergency dentist, family dentist). As you pick those words, you bid, and you pay on a per click basis.

So, let's just say you're bidding on the keywords "San Antonio Dentist," and there are a lot of other dentists in that city that want to rank for that keyword.

If you say that you'll pay $2.00/click and your competitor says that they'll pay $5.00/click, they're going to be at the top. Assuming nobody else has placed a higher bid, $2.00 is going to be ranked second and $1.20 is going to follow.

I am about to explain why that isn't 100% of the reality. The fact is that you pay on per click basis and you are bidding against the competitors to determine how you're going to rank on your keyword.

It's an auction, just like eBay. People are bidding and whoever can offer the most money is going to have the strong position. With that foundational understanding, we can now explain why most pay per click campaigns fail.

What tends to happen is a lot of pay per click campaigns are built on the notion that the highest bid wins. So, advertisers pick their keywords, throw up the highest bid per click and hope that everything turns out the way they want it.

Why Most Pay-Per-Click Campaigns Fail

- Setup only one ad group for all services
- Don't use specific text ads and landing pages for groups of keywords
- No strong call to action or OFFER on the landing page

You might be thinking, you just told me that PPC is a great way to get noticed, and now you're saying that most campaigns fail! I'm going to explain what people do wrong and then show you what to do right so that your campaign is successful.

Typically, businesses setup only one ad group for all services, whether it's assisted living facility, memory care home, independent living, senior living community, etc. instead of different ad groups for each type of service.

Also, there's no specific text ads and no landing pages for those ad groups and groups of keywords.

What you wind up with is the same landing page and the same text ad, whether your customer typed in "assisted living facility, memory care home, independent living, senior living community, etc." in the search engine.

Whatever was typed into the search engine was likely very specific, and should match up to a very specific page, but that doesn't happen. It all goes to the home page. With this strategy, not only is your campaign going to convert poorly, but your cost per click is going to be higher. I will explain why later in this chapter.

The other reason why most pay per click campaigns fail is because there isn't a strong call-to-action on the landing page. So, you were just charged $5.00 or $9.00 to get a potential customer to your website and the page isn't even compelling because it does not have a strong call-to-action. It doesn't tell the consumer what to do next.

If you factor these common reasons that pay per click campaigns tend to fail, you can better prepare yourself and set yourself up for success in the way that you execute your pay per click marketing.

Understanding the AdWords Auction Process

Let's talk about how the Google Ads Auction process works. It's not as simple as the highest bidder winning. It's more complicated than that.

The reality is Google needs to feature the most relevant results because their endgame is to get people to keep using their search engine over the competition. This is how they can keep their traffic up.

Google can keep their usage up and maintain that 80 percent market share but can also run Ads and make billions of dollars per year. Ultimately it all comes down to relevancy.

The second they sacrifice relevancy for dollars, is the second they start to become less of a player in their market. So, Google had to figure out a way to make their pay per click program grow around relevancy. And so that's why they established the quality score. They need to make sure that the person or company who has more relevancy gets a higher quality score and as result, can have a lower cost per click.

The way I like to explain it is, if I go to Google and I type in "BMW," obviously I am looking for a BMW dealer or for information about BMW.

Mercedes could say, "That's our demographic also. If someone types in BMW, they're looking for a high-end vehicle. They are probably in the market to buy. Why don't I bid on the word BMW?" Of course, they can. However, the person that searched BMW isn't looking for Mercedes. So, Mercedes could say, "I'll pay $25.00 for everybody that clicks on me when they search 'BMW'."

But BMW might say, "That's my brand and I am going to compete for it, but I am not going to spend $25.00 for every click on my own brand. I'll pay a dollar for every click." Based on quality score, Google may decide to serve BMW because it's in the best interest of the person researching the brand, the consumer. It's also in the best interest of overall relevancy. That's how quality score works. Quality score is really driven by three core components:

1. Click thru rate
2. Relevance
3. Quality of the Landing Page

As somebody conducts a search and your website shows up on the page in the pay per click section, Google is tracking what percentage of those people saw your ad and wound up clicking through.

That's one of the primary metrics that they analyze. So, if your ad is relevant, if it speaks to the person's needs, and if it's compelling enough to them that they click through, Google just made more per click.

This will make them willing to give you a higher quality score because you've got better click-through rate.

Also, relevancy is a major factor. How relevant is your text ad to the keyword that was typed?

Example: If they type in "senor care," and your text ad reads: "We're the best Senor Care home in the Dallas area," versus "We're the best Senor Care home in the Dallas area and we offer 24/7 nursing in the Dallas area."

Which do you think is more relevant to the customer? Google wants their search results to be as applicable as possible. They're looking at your click-through rate, they are looking at the relevancy of your text ad to your keywords, and they are looking at the quality of your landing page.

If your landing page (the page that you drive people to) doesn't match up with what the person just clicked based on your text ad, or if that landing page doesn't have a strong call-to-action and the person quickly returns to the search engine, that signals to Google that you were not very relevant.

This will result in a quality score reduction.

By having a higher quality score, you can bid lower and still achieve the top position. This is where you can win in the pay per click marketing game because a better-quality score results in a lower cost-per-click for those who hold the top positions.

Again, if we just look at the reason most pay per click campaigns fail, it's because:

- You only set up one ad group
- You had the opportunity to create a separate ad group for each one of your core services, but you don't use a specific text ad that's going to compel someone to click and improve your click-through rate
- You don't have a strong call-to-action that matches up with what the consumer was looking for
- You're not going to have high click-through rate, relevancy, or an applicable landing page

All of these issues result in a lower quality score.

You're going to wind up paying more per click. PPC marketing is very competitive. If you're paying more per click, you're not going to be able to spend that much because you won't be getting enough calls to generate return on investment.

The visual representation of this would be like setting up one AdWords campaign for each one of these services (dentist, emergency dentist, family dentistry, cosmetic dentistry, teeth cleaning, dental braces, etc.) and landing people on your home page. That is a recipe for disaster.

That's exactly what you don't want to do.

How to setup your PPC campaign for success

Let's talk about how to position your pay per click campaign for success.

What can you do to ensure the highest probability of success in your pay per click campaign? For starters, set up ad groups based on the specific groups of services that you offer (we're going to map this out using a variety of businesses as an example).

Write compelling text ads that are relevant to your specific keywords or services. Then, link your ads to the specific pages on your site rather than the home page. But, the specific pages on your site that talk about that service should have a strong call-to-action combined with an offer.

What ad groups should you use? What ad groups do you need to set up for your business? Using a dental clinic company as   an   example:

- Assisted Living
- Memory Care
- Independent living
- Senior community
- Adult day care

If you are in the Senor care business, you need to have standard senor care for the general, "I need a senor care home," or "I'm looking for a senor home" search. They didn't get very specific. You should have something for that. Have assisted living facility available, for the person who types in "assisted living facility near met," "assisted living facility," "24-hour assisted living," etc. You want to group those keywords together and have information available for that.

We could go a lot deeper than this, but you should have an idea of what specific types of ad groups you need to set up based on the services you offer. From there, you want to write a specific text ad that speaks to that group of keywords.

Then, you will want to drive them to a landing page on your website that has a compelling call-to-action, that provides what they were looking for and mirrors what your text ad said. I've got a template below to review:

- Pick your list of keywords
- Write a specific text ad that matches up with what those people are looking for
- Drive them to a landing page on your website

Make sure that you've got compelling content on that landing page that emphasizes what they were looking for and prompts them into action, ideally with some type of coupon or special offer, so that they don't move beyond your page and keep looking around.

Educate and Engage

Why would they want to choose your company versus the competition? This is where you'd want to play up your authority in Senor care. If you've been caring for Senors for over 25 years… then make sure you say that. If you've won awards… make sure you say that… with the caveat that you ALWAYS say those things with empathy for where the consumer is in their life journey. Remember, they are either looking for their last home for themselves or their parents.

On the landing page, you can really position yourself and educate them in a way that will make them want to choose your facility.

You can also use email marketing to send them messages over time. If they're at the beginning of their serach, you do your best to catch them early. Maybe it's going to be six months before they decide to make the final decision or to move forward with any type of move.

Because you got their email you could send them one email per week for the next six months. They're going to get something new from you once a week. Nothing annoying, but, "Here's an update, here's another thing, here's another interesting concept you can look at".

When they do get to the point that they are ready to move forward, they've seen you so many times and you've added so much value that they have no choice but to choose your company. You've made the decision easy for them.

This is a way to position yourself better for the longer purchase cycle projects, so you can capture more leads and convert them into customers.

AdWords Setup Best Practices

Here are some best practices when you get into Google Ads (ads.google.com).

The first one is that you want to make sure you set up an extension with your address.

In chapter one, we showed you how to set up your Google Business Profiel and optimize it to rank in the Google Map 3 Pack. You want to use the same Gmail account that you claimed your map listing with on Google Ads, so that you can come into extensions and add your address as an extension.

This gives you the ability to add your address and a direct link to your Google Business Profile listing in your search.

In the screenshot above, you can see the ads for two Hail Damage Repair service providers. Not only do they have their text ad, but they've also got additional extensions on the ad with important site links, a link to their Google Business Profile listing and their address. Can you see how that pops off these two ads a little more than the others? This is something you definitely want to consider. You want to take the time to set up your Ads extensions.

Have Multiple Text Ads for Each Ad Group and Run Split Tests

The other best practice is to have multiple text ads for every one of your ad groups. This way, you can split test and see each of your ads and determine which one is converting better.

For example, split test by looking at these two ads for Steak Restaurant. They're just different variations of the same messaging. They're going to get equal share. If there are one thousand impressions, you could distribute 500 to one and 500 to the other.

AdWords Best Practices
Have Multiple Versions of your Ads and Split Test for best CTR

Ad	Status	↓ Clicks	Impr.	CTR	Avg. CPC
Steakhouse 35Day Dry Aged Beef | Breathtaking dining room landingpage.zprime.com Best Steak Restaurant located in the heart of White Plains, NY. Easily Accessible from Westchester and Surrounding Areas. Reserve now online.	Campaign paused	241	13,010	1.85%	CA$1.99
Steak Restaurant White Plains | High Quality Dining Experience landingpage.zprime.com Dine Like Royalty at the New Z Prime Italian Steakhouse. Best Steak Restaurant Westchester. Comfortable lounge area. Open for Dinner. Mon - Sat. Easily...	Campaign paused	79	3,755	2.10%	CA$2.46
Best Italian Steak Restaurant | Get A $20 Gift Certificate landingpage.zprime.com Dine Like Royalty at Z Prime Steakhouse. Bar and Lounge area. Open for Dinner. Mon - Sat. Breathtaking dining room. Luxurious Bar and Lounge area. Open for Dinner. Mon	Campaign paused	46	5,972	0.77%	CA$1.76

By split testing, you will be able to determine which one had a higher click-through rate. With that information, you can drop out the lower performing ad and create a new one.

Then at the end of the month, you can compare those two ads and see which one performed better. You keep doing that so you can continually improve your click-through ratios.

Remember, having better click-through rates is going to get you more traffic, but it's also going to give you a better-quality score. This will eventually make your cost-per-click lower, making it more profitable for you in the long-term.

Pay Attention to Average Position

Ad group	Status	Default Max. CPC	Clicks ↓	Impr.	CTR	Avg. CPC	Cost	Avg. Pos.
Total - all ad groups			1,933	171,421	1.13%		$3.43	1.1
Social Media Marketing		$18.25	860	13,556	6.34%		$1.09	1.1
Email Marketing		$19.75	200	20,338	0.98%		$3.14	1.1
Website Design		$19.75	140	20,062	0.70%		$9.98	1.2
Web Design		$19.75	117	27,831	0.42%		$6.32	1.1
Social Media Advertising		$14.75	92	15,821	0.58%		$2.06	1.0

The other thing you want to do is to pay attention to your average position in your Google Ads campaign. These settings are available making it very easy to analyze the data.

In the report above, you can see what position is being maintained. The average position is highlighted. This is based on the quality score and the average cost per click. You want to maintain a top four position on the major search engines in your pay per click marketing campaign.

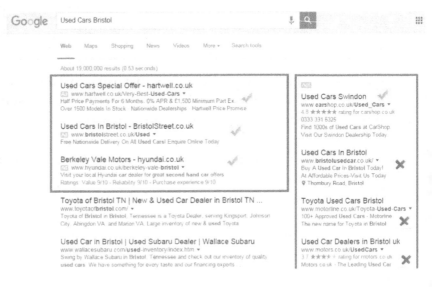

We have found that the further down the list they go, the higher the probability that you will be attracting a price shopper that's literally clicking every single company along the way.

You don't necessarily need to be the top listing, because that could just be a result of some random person that didn't think through what they're doing.

However, you want to maintain a top four position. That's going to give you the best overall visibility, and ultimately, the best return on your investment.

Pay attention to your average cost-per-click and manage your bids so you maintain a top four position.

Exact Match versus Broad Match

The other thing you want to pay attention to is exact match versus broad match.

You have a setting inside your AdWords campaign where you specify whether you want exact match or broad match.

Always Elect to do Exact Match

The reason is because if you choose broad match, you could very easily find yourself accidentally showing up on the search engines for a lot of keywords that have nothing to do with your specific business.

The other thing you want to do is pay attention to negative keywords – keywords that you don't want to show up for in the search engine.

A great example of this is jobs, employment, marketing, etc.

If someone types in "your city assisted living facility," that's great. If they type in "your city assisted living facility jobs," that's somebody looking for employment in the ALF industry. Unless you are trying to fill a position or if you actually want to use your pay per click budget to get applicants, it's probably not the kind of the person you want to attract.

Setting up negative keywords means, for example, if someone types in "jobs," "employment," or "marketing services" anywhere in their search, it pulls you out of that search.

It pulls you out of that specific bidding process, so you won't be paying for clicks from somebody that's not relevant to you.

Mobile PPC

I talked a little bit about making sure that you've set up mobile pay per click campaigns. I've mentioned the major transition of people searching on their mobile device versus people searching on their computer.

Phone Searches versus Computer Searches

More and more people are accessing the Internet via smart devices: their iPhone, Android, and tablets. The searcher is typically in a different mind-frame when they are searching from a phone rather than from the computer.

When you're searching from a phone, you often just want to get the information right away, and/or want your problem solved as soon as possible. You can set up a campaign to have click-to-call built into your mobile campaign.

If somebody hits that "Call" button, they're connected immediately to that business. This is a quick alternative to having to search for the website and the phone number on your own. Plus, you can see on a mobile phone there is not a lot of screen space.

Those pay per click listings become really prominent and they dominate the search results page on mobile. A lot of times, you're going to get the majority of the clicks if you're in those top two positions. It's all about convenience, and the click-to-call function allows that.

It's extremely powerful to connect with these people that are searching from mobile devices. Set up a mobile-specific campaign and choose "Mobile Devices Only." Then you can pick your geolocation. That would be your 30-mile range or 20-mile radius. You then click a button to turn on the click-to-call function.

That's how you wind up with a pay per click campaign that has you in the top positions if you bid correctly, with the options for them to do a click-to-call.

Just to recap, you want to:

- Set up your ad groups correctly
- Make sure that you pick keywords that group them together
- You write text ads that speak directly to that group of keywords, and
- Ensure your landing page (where you are sending those specific searches) speaks to the text ads and the group of keywords
- You also want to be sure that you have some type of strong call-to-action that prompts your consumer into calling you as opposed to pressing the "Back" button and looking at four or five other competitors

As the relevancy of your ad groups campaign and your keywords improve, your cost-per-click will decline and your conversion will improve.

You can spend less and still get better positioning and more traffic to your website. This is how you maximize the profitability of your pay-per-click marketing campaigns an succeed in PPC where others fail.

12 PAID ONLINE DIRECTORIES

In this chapter, we're going to be covering paid online directory listings.

We talked about the overall Internet market strategy, beginning with the foundation of having a properly optimized website. We have also discussed making sure that you've got yourself set up with all the right pages on your website, the conversion elements, doing the off page optimization for building inbound links, building authority for your domain, having the review acquisition strategy, and making sure that you're ranking in the organic, non-pay-per-click listings for your most important keywords.

We then talked about looking at social media and email marketing as a way to connect with your customer on a deeper level and get more repeated referral business. As you get those non-paid elements of your Internet marketing strategy squared away, you can start looking at paid online marketing programs.

We talked about pay-per-click marketing, and the way you could set up an effective pay-per-click marketing campaign on AdWords or Microsoft Bing search in order to show up in the paid listings.

In this chapter, I want to talk about other paid marketing components, such as online directory listings that you can pay for to get premium listings.

There are literally hundreds of online directories, from Yelp.com and Foursquare, to City Search, and BBB, as well as an array of smaller secondary directories. I'm going to talk about the ones that are the biggest; the ones that will help you gain exposure where your customers are looking most.

Paid Online Directory Listings and Online Sites You Should Consider

As mentioned, there are literally hundreds of online directory listings. The ones that we have found to be the most prominent and   visited   are:

- Yelp
- Yellow Pages
- Foursquare
- BBBMerchant   Circle

If you have an unlimited budget and you are already doing well with your organics, and you wanted to pay for some additional premium placement in online directories, these are the ones I would suggest that you take into consideration.

yelp.com

Yelp is one of the best review sites for local businesses. If you want customers to find your business online, you need to be on Yelp. Yelp allows you to send public or private messages (including deals) to customers and review business trends using the Yelp reporting tool. If, for some reason, you have a lot of reviews on Yelp.com, it might not be a bad idea to pay for a premium ad on their directory for your services.

YP.com

The online yellow pages vary area by area. In some markets, it is YP.com and in others, it is DexKnows.com, Version Yellow Pages, YellowBook.com or some similar version.

With YP.com and other online yellow pages, you need to be very careful when you get started. You don't want to be roped into their print Yellow Page ad. The cost goes from a couple hundred bucks a month to potentially a couple thousand dollars per month when you start to get into their Yellow Pages book and their pay-per-click advertising.

Do not let Yellow Pages manage your pay-per-click advertising under any circumstances. There is a whole chapter on Pay-Per-Click Marketing in this book. I go into great depth about how to set up an effective pay-per-click campaign. You don't want to let any of these companies try and touch your pay-per-click advertising on Google, Yahoo or Bing. Do it the right way. Set up the ad groups on your own.

City Search

City Search specializes in listings for restaurants, bars, spas, hotels, restaurants, and other businesses across the U.S., optimizing them via a partner network that includes Expedia and MerchantCircle.

Better Business Bureau

BBB, the Better Business Bureau is not just an online directory, it is a major sign of credibility. It's not as popular as it once was but posting the BBB logo and being able to say that you're A+ credited is worth the investment. I haven't found that it allows for a ton of leads, but it's a great credibility symbol and a good thing to be able to reference.

Foursquare

Foursquare is nowhere near as popular as Yelp, but it does provide listings for all kinds of local businesses. 93 percent of local storefronts represent 2 million of the businesses who are already listed on Foursquare, and the site is visited by more than 50 million people.

MerchantCircle

MerchantCircle allows people to find the best local merchants. The site includes listings for all kinds of merchants and business owners, ranging from attorneys and notaries to realtors and agencies. Over 100 million consumers visited the site last year to search its listings of 2 million businesses. The site gets around 340,000 monthly visits.

13 TRACK, MEASURE, & QUANTIFY

Congratulations!   Now   That   You   Have...

- Built and optimized your website
- An ongoing link building strategy in place where you're creating inbound links and moving up in the search engines
- Implemented email marketing and social media marketing initiatives, and
- Possibly implemented a paid online marketing campaign including Pay-Per-Click and Pay-Per-Lead services...

...You need to put some tools in place so that you can track, measure and quantify your data to ensure that you're moving in a positive direction.

Analytics   Tracking

There are a lot of different tracking mechanisms that you can put in place. I'm going to recommend three core tracking mechanisms:

- Google Analytics
- Keyword Tracking
- Call   Tracking

The first is Google Analytics. Google Analytics is a great

website data analysis tool and it's completely free. Googl
Analytics will show you specificall

- How many visitors got to your website on a dail
weekly, monthly, and annual bas

- What keywords they typed in to get there
- What pages on your website they visited
- How long they staye

The main thing you want to see from Google Analytics
where you started and where you are now.

You want to ask yourself: When I started this whole Intern
marketing process, how many visitors was I getting to m
website? Maybe it was 5, 20, 100, or 500, but it's good to knov
Then you can compare to future data on an ongoing basis.

Ultimately, what you are looking for is whether or not th
number of visitors to your website is increasing. Is the variety o
keywords that they're finding you with increasing? Are yo
moving in a positive direction?

You can also set up reports within Google Analytics. To g
set up on Google Analytics, you just go t
Google.com/analytics. It's a simple process. You verify that yo
own the website through a variety of different methods, an
then install a small piece of code into your website's HTMI
After you have done that, you've got the tracking in place an
are ready to go.

Google Analytics Reports

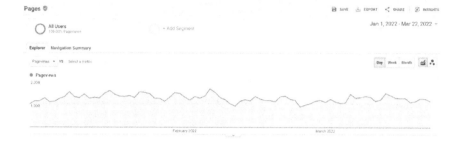

All pages and traffic, year to date

Traffic by Top Pages

	Page	Pageviews ↓	Unique Pageviews	Avg. Time on Page	Entrances	Bounce Rate
		99,013 % of Total: 100.00% (99,013)	**45,030** % of Total: 100.00% (45,030)	**00:00:31** Avg for View: 00:00:31 (0.00%)	**43,223** % of Total: 100.00% (43,223)	**0.57%** Avg for View: 0.57% (0.00%)
1.	/will-your-cell-phone-work-in-cancun-what-you-must-know/	**11,199** (11.31%)	5,235 (11.63%)	00:00:28	5,170 (11.96%)	0.33%
2.	/	**9,237** (9.33%)	3,874 (8.60%)	00:00:28	3,398 (7.86%)	4.59%
3.	/can-you-get-to-cancun-without-flying-yes-heres-how/	**8,181** (8.26%)	3,724 (8.27%)	00:00:29	3,710 (8.58%)	0.19%
4.	/cancun-should-you-go-all-inclusive-the-pros-and-cons/	**5,718** (5.77%)	2,469 (5.48%)	00:00:57	2,443 (5.65%)	0.16%
5.	/bugs-and-insects-in-cancun-should-you-be-worried/	**5,295** (5.35%)	2,481 (5.51%)	00:00:22	2,470 (5.71%)	0.24%
6.	/are-there-sharks-in-cancun-heres-the-truth/	**5,067** (5.12%)	2,377 (5.28%)	00:00:25	2,368 (5.48%)	0.13%
7.	/can-you-take-shells-home-from-cancun/	**4,965** (5.01%)	2,317 (5.15%)	00:00:25	2,311 (5.35%)	0.17%
8.	/is-cancun-est-or-cst/	**4,754** (4.80%)	2,220 (4.93%)	00:00:28	2,219 (5.13%)	0.09%
9.	/how-to-avoid-spring-breakers-in-cancun/	**4,689** (4.74%)	2,188 (4.86%)	00:00:35	2,180 (5.04%)	0.14%
10.	/do-cancun-resorts-have-us-outlets/	**3,970** (4.01%)	1,884 (4.18%)	00:00:25	1,875 (4.34%)	0.27%

By Device

Mobile Device Info		Acquisition					Behavior
		Users ↓		New Users		Sessions	Bounce Rate
		27,559 % of Total: 73.58% (37,453)		**27,096** % of Total: 73.37% (36,933)		**32,474** % of Total: 75.13% (43,223)	**0.66%** Avg for View: 0.57% (16.33%)
1.	Apple iPhone	**19,625**	(71.90%)	19,448	(71.77%)	23,979 (73.84%)	0.75%
2.	Apple iPad	**495**	(1.81%)	495	(1.83%)	563 (1.73%)	0.18%
3.	Samsung SM-G991U Galaxy S21 5G	**277**	(1.01%)	277	(1.02%)	303 (0.93%)	0.33%
4.	(not set)	**261**	(0.96%)	261	(0.96%)	297 (0.91%)	0.00%
5.	Samsung SM-G998U Galaxy S21 Ultra 5G	**236**	(0.86%)	236	(0.87%)	257 (0.79%)	0.39%
6.	Samsung SM-G973U Galaxy S10	**187**	(0.69%)	187	(0.69%)	204 (0.63%)	0.49%
7.	Samsung SM-G960U Galaxy S9	**166**	(0.61%)	167	(0.62%)	183 (0.56%)	0.00%
8.	Samsung SM-G975U Galaxy S10+	**128**	(0.47%)	128	(0.47%)	157 (0.48%)	0.64%
9.	Samsung SM-G970U Galaxy S10e	**125**	(0.46%)	125	(0.46%)	148 (0.46%)	1.35%
10.	Samsung SM-G965U Galaxy S9+	**104**	(0.38%)	104	(0.38%)	115 (0.35%)	0.87%

Behavior Flow

Behavior Flow

Jan 1, 2022 - Ma

Automatically Grouped Pages ▾   Level of Detail ▾   Export ▾

All Users
100.00% Sessions

+ Add Segment

Keyword Tracking

The other tracking mechanism that I recommend is keyword tracking. At the beginning of this process, we talked about keyword research to determine what keywords people are typing in when they need your services.

We came up with a list and all those keywords were combined with your cities and sub-cities.

There are tools that will tell you how you're ranking on Google, Yahoo, and Bing for those various keywords. A few options include:

- Bright Local
- White Spark
- Raven Tools

The keyword tracking tool I recommend is called BrightLocal.

You can learn more about it at brightlocal.com. There is a cost associated with this service, but it is great resource for tracking your search engine optimization progress.

You take your keywords, put them into the BrightLocal Keyword Tracker and then set up a weekly and monthly report that shows where you rank on Google, Yahoo and Bing for your most important keywords.

Brightlocal has a host of other tracking tools that are very valuable for a local business. They can now track how you're ranking within a small radius of your business on local, and display that on a grid. This will also show you who is ranking #1 instead of you.

Overall Top Ranking Competitors for 'upscale assisted living dallas'
Top-performing search results competitors, based on the Grid Points for this keyword.

Here's an example of the grid report.

With a report like this, you can easily see how your website is trending in the search engines.

You'll see yourself move up in the results if you've built out the website correctly with the right on-page factors (title tags, H1 tags, meta descriptions, etc.), if you're building links, developing citations and have a proactive review acquisition system in place.

If you see yourself stagnating, you can go back to that keyword, figure out which page is optimized for it, look at your links and link profile, and whatever is necessary to push that keyword to the next level.

Call Tracking

The third really important tracking mechanism that I recommend is call tracking. Having better rankings and more visits to your website is all fine and dandy, but in most businesses, nothing happens until a call is made.

Calls are crucial to your business. You want to have some type of tracking mechanism in place to know how many calls are coming in on a monthly basis and what's happening within those conversations.

Are calls turning into sales? That's where the rubber meets the road. That's why we're doing all of this. Who cares if you're in the number one position if it doesn't result in dollars to the business?

There are several call tracking tools that you can use. Here are a few:
- CallFire
- DialogTech
- CallSource
- Century   Interactive

One of the tools I've seen used prevalently is called CallFire. You can learn more about it at www.CallFire.com.

Most of these call tracking services will let you choose a phone number based on your area code. So, you type in the number you want to get. It's a nominal fee on a monthly basis ($2 - $5 per month), and you get a tracking number.

Then, you can take that tracking phone number and you can

put it on the graphics on your website so that you can track th number of calls and even listen to recordings of th conversation.

That number will be set to ring in your office. It's just forwarding number. If somebody dials it, it still rings to you office like always, but it is a tracking number.

You can report on the number of calls using the Internet and play back recordings of those conversations. It's extremely powerful to know the number of calls you were getting when you started versus the number after you incorporated your new marketing strategy.

You can go in and listen to those conversations and ascertain how many of those calls turned into booked service while knowing what the revenue associated with that service is. That is how you get a true gauge on the return on investment associated with your online marketing strategy.

These are the types of tracking mechanisms I recommend. There are a lot of different things you can do, but having analytics, keyword tracking, and call tracking really gives you the most important key performance indicators to gauge your progress.

14 WHAT'S NEXT

Throughout the course of this book, we have covered an abundance of information.

We've mapped out your Internet marketing plan and taken you step-by-step through how to claim and optimize your Google map listing, how to optimize your website for the most commonly searched keywords in your area and how to leverage social media to get more repeat and referral business.

We then covered paid online marketing strategies like pay-per-click and pay-per-lead services. If you have taken action and followed our instructions, you should be well on your way to dominating the search engines for the keywords in your area.

Need More Help?

If you've gotten to this point and feel like you need some extra help to implement these ideas, we are here to support you. As experts in helping online businesses across the nation, we have had tremendous success implementing these strategies.

You can call us directly at 817-904-5080 with any questions that you might have. Our team will review your entire online marketing effort (Website, Competition, Search Engine Placement, Social Media, etc.) and come back to you with a complete assessment of how you can improve and what you can do to take your online marketing efforts to the next level.

Request A Free Custom Online Marketing Evaluation Now

Your Custom-Tailored Optimization Audit will:

- Identify key issues that could be harming your website without you even knowing it.
- Look at where your website stands compared to your competitors.
- Determine whether SEO is the appropriate route for you to take.
- Uncover hidden revenue that you're leaving on the table.
- Offer recommendations that you can put to use immediately

Schedule your custom audit at https://avetamarketing.com/

ABOUT THE AUTHOR

Mitch Alverson is the founder and CEO of Aveta Marketing. Aveta Marketing exists to help Assisted Living Facilities and Senior Housing Communities get their online marketing right so that Seniors find the best places to live. Mitch believes that when ALFs thrive, Seniors get better care.

Mitch is a graduate of Dallas Baptist University and The University of Texas at Arlington. He holds a Masters of Business Administration and Bachelor's degree of Arts and Science. Mitch is also a Lean Six Sigma Master Black Belt and studied at General Electric and the Lasater Institute in Indiana.

Mitch has been a StoryBrand Certified Guide since 2017 and a Certified Business Made Simple Coach since 2020.

Mitch lives in Arlington, Texas with his family and enjoys traveling and coaching his son's baseball team. His favorite travel destination is Cancun, Mexico and he and his wife Michele have a travel blog and you can read it at cancunareatravel.com

Made in the USA
Las Vegas, NV
04 January 2024

83828895R00085